DO JUSTICE,
LOVE MERCY,
WALK HUMBLY

DO JUSTICE, LOVE MERCY, WALK HUMBLY

A Biography of the Honorable Vernon J. Ehlers

Julia R. LaPlaca

Published 2017 by the Vernon J. Ehlers Family
1837 Plymouth Terrace SE
Grand Rapids, MI 49506

Scripture quotations marked RSV are taken from the Revised Standard Version of the Bible, copyright © 1946, 1952, and 1971 the Division of Christian Education of the National Council of the Churches of Christ in the United States of America. Used by permission. All rights reserved.

Published and printed in the United States of America by
The family of Vernon J. Ehlers

Publisher's Cataloging-in-Publication data
Names: LaPlaca, Julia R., author.
Title: Do Justice, Love Mercy, Walk Humbly: A Biography of the Honorable Vernon J. Ehlers / by Julia R. LaPlaca.
Description: Includes bibliographical references. | Grand Rapids, MI: Family of Vernon J. Ehlers, 2017.
Identifiers: ISBN: 978-1-937555-98-6 | LCCN: 2017912371
Subjects: Ehlers, Vernon J., (1934–2017) | BISAC BIOGRAPHY & AUTOBIOGRAPHY / Political | POLITICAL SCIENCE / American Government / General

Cover design: Victoria Seaburg
Interior design and layout: VictoriaSeaburg@gmail.com

Table of Contents

Sine qua non

We wish to acknowledge the contributions of the following indispensable persons without whom this book would not have been possible:

Matt Walhout. Matt Walhout was the first to recognize that Vern's story was one worth telling—and to make work of it. Without Matt's vision, this book would have remained unwritten, buried in tidy numbered boxes in the Calvin College archives. A fellow physicist with an appreciation of the importance of engaging in the political arena, Matt worked tirelessly to make sure that Vern's legacy would be recorded.

Julia LaPlaca. Although Julia began working on this project because she needed a job (her words), she threw herself into it with grace and style. She combed through all those tidy numbered boxes in the archives (as well as a daunting number of untidy boxes) and interviewed key people in Vern's life, and from those threads wove together a fascinating tale. Her gift of storytelling has documented Vern's life so compellingly that the reader can't help but love and be inspired by the nerdy politician.

Dale Williams, **Steve Kline**, **Victoria Seaburg**. This dream team of a production manager, copy editor, and designer managed to turn a simple manuscript into the book before you. Their combined talents and cheerful willingness to burn the midnight oil were a true blessing.

Jo Ehlers. Throughout their 59 years of marriage, Jo was the vital pillar of support who made Vern's personal and professional achievements possible. Although frequently visible by Vern's side at key moments throughout his career, Jo's greatest contribution was behind the scenes and out of the public's sight. Jo was the loving mother of their four children (Heidi, Brian, Marla, and Todd) and dedicated herself to raising them with the Christian values Vern and Jo both held so dear. Jo created a warm and supportive home for Vern to retreat to, as he did nearly every weekend throughout his tenure in Congress. Jo selflessly supported Vern's decisions to advance through political positions because, as she often commented, "he's doing so much good for the world, it's important he continue doing it as long as God allows him to."

To each of these dear people we are deeply indebted and eternally grateful.

Thank you.

The Vernon J. Ehlers Family

August 2017

Preface

Although I had caught a train at the Vernon J. Ehlers Amtrak station and glimpsed the Thursday drink special, "The Vern Ehlers," advertised at a Grand Rapids bar, I hadn't really *heard* of Vern Ehlers until one of my professors at Calvin, Matt Walhout, asked whether I wanted a summer job going through Vern's archive at Calvin College.

I did need a job. So I jumped into a couple dozen boxes of Vern's unsorted papers and his catalogued archive at Calvin College. Vern's story takes some interesting turns: pranks at Calvin College from its Franklin Campus days, physics research at Berkeley circa 1963, the birth of the environmental movement and solid-waste disposal disputes in Kent County in the 1970s, wetlands protection in Michigan in the 1980s, the Republican Party's rise to a congressional majority in the 1990s, the upheavals in the Middle East of the early 2000s, and the financial crisis of 2008.

I also learned about Vern Ehlers the person. Judging by the number of newspaper clippings, itineraries, letters, memos, class notes, lectures, speeches, bill drafts, and news releases, I quickly discovered that he was quite a saver.

He thought through problems with confidence and logic. He possessed a strong sense of duty to love and care for the world. He loved a good pun; he relished his time as a professor. He thought about all kinds of problems and wanted to solve them with the utmost efficiency, thoroughness, and frugality (he was Dutch, after all). He loved his family. He was a great boss. He loved science and was inspired by how understanding the intricacies of creation reveals completely new ways of interacting with the world.

The account of Ehlers's life presented here is superficial at best. As neither a politician nor a scientist, I can't offer a nuanced view of Ehlers's work. However, I have tried to present a true account of his life and the motivations he had for entering into politics by highlighting episodes in his story that I found important or interesting. My judgment was aided first by Matt Walhout, also a professor of physics, who had first expressed an interest in studying Ehlers. He oversaw the first leg of the archival research and helped with the editing of this short book. Interviews with people who knew Ehlers well—his family, former staffers, friends, and colleagues—helped me decide what to include in this story.

Vern's life of service serves as a profound example of what Christian public service looks like. People remember his kindness and unashamed nerdiness. They also remember how hard he worked. Ehlers made time for his constituents; he could readily explain his votes, because his decision making was based on hard logic. He took the opinions of experts very seriously when it came to scientific questions, because he was an expert in some of these areas too. He worked hard because he wanted to help people. His integrity offers a model of what is possible, though perhaps less common, in politics today.

Spending so much time in Vern's thoughts this year has made me both nostalgic and hopeful. There is a deep potential for good in government, amid the troubling obstacles and injustices. Vern had that redemptive vision of the good, and, rather than getting cynical, he got busy following it.

I come away from this project a wiser, more thankful, and more inspired citizen. I learned so much from Vern, and, who knows, maybe someday I'll pull a Vern Ehlers myself and run for a position in my own community. No matter that I didn't study political science, Vern's story demonstrates that government always needs people who can work hard and care deeply—leaders who step out of their comfort zone with integrity and a desire to pursue justice, love mercy, and walk humbly in their role as public servants. Vern Ehlers certainly did.

~ Julia LaPlaca

A Micah 6:8 Call

When Vernon J. Ehlers first ran for West Michigan's Kent County Commission, he was not your typical candidate. He was from rural Dutch stock in Edgerton, Minnesota, and hadn't attended school as a child because of poor health. Decades later, this balding, asthmatic, forty-year-old, Berkeley-trained nuclear physicist, father of four, and college professor ran for office on the unlikely campaign platform of solid waste disposal. As a budding environmentalist, he understood this kind of issue best. Mild-mannered, determined, and smart as a whip, Ehlers approached the campaign with an uncanny dual penchant both for seeing big-picture strategies and for attending to nitty-gritty details. Building upon the details immediately before him, Ehlers could envision and work toward bigger goals.

Vern Ehlers, 1974

In this first campaign, Ehlers knew his experience in the community would not be enough to win an election. He approached the problem with characteristic thoughtfulness and thoroughness. His activities at Eastern Avenue Christian Reformed Church and his committee work at Calvin College had honed his leadership skills; he had studied issues in his community and knew he could offer solutions. But he needed to make a name for himself. "More was needed than simply discussion of the issues," said Ehlers. In order to establish name identification, "I decided to distribute to each household in the district some small gift from

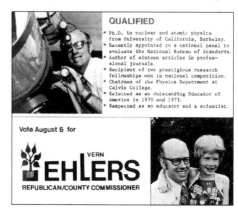

QUALIFIED

* Ph.D. in nuclear and atomic physics from University of California, Berkeley.
* Recently appointed to a national panel to evaluate the National Bureau of Standards.
* Author of sixteen articles in professional journals.
* Recipient of two prestigious research fellowships won in national competition.
* Chairman of the Physics Department at Calvin College.
* Selected as an Outstanding Educator of America in 1970 and 1973.
* Respected as an educator and a scientist.

Vote August 6 for

VERN
EHLERS
REPUBLICAN/COUNTY COMMISSIONER

County Commissioner campaign pamphlet, 1974

me . . . which would provide strong name identification. I further insisted that this gift be something useful, and not merely a trinket which would be thrown away."[1]

So Ehlers's team prepared 3,000 seedlings in cups which were labeled in green letters "Keep Kent County green—plant this tree and vote for Vern Ehlers." He planned the initiative to the last detail, even making sure that planting instructions came with each seedling. In keeping with his campaign's theme, "Spruce up Kent County" (not to mention his personal fondness for puns), the seedlings were of course spruces. Once the seedlings had been planted and the votes cast,

Vern and children hand out spruce trees during the 1974 primary campaign for the Kent County Board of Commissioners.

Ehlers was elected to the Kent County Commission in 1974. It was truly an Ehlers-style campaign: thrifty, efficient, eco-friendly, and well planned.

From the county commission, Ehlers embarked on a remarkable climb up the political ladder. He moved from county politics into the state House, then state Senate, and finally to the United States Congress, where he served Michigan's third district from 1993 to 2011.

At every level of government, Ehlers's training as a scientist made him unique. As he liked to tell reporters, he was the "first physicist ever elected to the U.S. Congress and the first at this level of government since Ben Franklin."[2] Members of the scientific community were surprised at the career switch from academia into public service, but Ehlers's "nerd" status was perhaps his biggest asset. He wrote, "There are so many technical and scientific issues to be dealt with today in the legislative arena, and most members have little to no knowledge about them."[3] Cloning, climate change, nuclear missiles, ozone layer depletion,

Vern and Jo Ehlers, President George W. Bush and First Lady Laura Bush, December 3, 2001.
Ehlers served during the Clinton, Bush, and Obama terms.

invasive species, oil drilling, the science budget, and a host of other issues rose to the forefront in late twentieth and early twenty-first centuries. During his lengthy career as a legislator, Ehlers faced them all. His status as a scientist gave his opinion weight. He often found himself in an advisory role in Congress, as he could explain scientific processes and clarify scientific concerns. As a policy maker, he stuck to his strengths: long-term infrastructure, science and technology, and STEM (science, technology, engineering, and mathematics) education legislation.

Ehlers exhibited the makings of scientist-politician long before he had any thought of entering politics. His attention to details, desire to problem solve, and love of discussing complex issues were evident in his early professional career.

Most importantly, it was Ehlers's faith that finally led him into politics. One particular Bible verse, Micah 6:8, animated his career:

> He has shown you, O man, what is good;
>   and what does the LORD require of you
> but to do justice, and to love mercy,
> and to walk humbly with your God? (RSV)

This verse hung in a place of prominence in all his various political offices. At every swearing-in ceremony, he placed his hand on an open Bible on these particular words. Ehlers felt a deep sense of responsibility to do justice in the world within the specific interests and skills God had given him. His sense of justice led him to advocate for the environment and get involved in his community. A love of mercy prompted the approaches he took to difficult legislation, and the desire to walk humbly guided his interactions with his constituents.

In this account of Ehlers's life, these Micah 6:8 principles appear often, beginning with the development of Ehlers's worldview in his childhood and at college. Ehlers is a fine example of what specifically Reformed Christian politics looks like in action. Ehlers brought a unique set of skills to his Micah 6:8 principles, which prepared him to flourish as a politician. Throughout his time in office, three policy areas were always close to Ehlers's heart: environmental protection, science policy, and education. He developed a passion for each of these early in his life, and he fought for them as politician, drawing on his intellect, energy, and Christian duty to care for the world.

CHAPTER ONE
Developing a Reformed Christian Perspective

Throughout his career, Ehlers insisted that he never had expected to run for political office. "In fact," said Ehlers to a reporter in 1994, "I didn't ever dream of becoming president when I was a kid, and I think most kids do."[4]

Ehlers was a well-trained physicist; he certainly could have pursued a career in research or a position as an academic administrator.[5] His skills were versatile. But Ehlers always had a strong desire to use his scientific know-how in service. In the end, it was Ehlers's Christian conviction to pursue justice and mercy that led him into public service.

Ehlers was a born-and-bred member of the Christian Reformed Church, a denomination that originated in West Michigan. In 1857, a small segment of the Dutch immigrant population in West Michigan split from the Reformed Church of America (then known as the Dutch Reformed Church) to form the Christian Reformed Church (CRC). The denomination, still headquartered in West Michigan, adheres to the Apostle's, Nicene, and Athanasian Creeds, as well as three other confessions; nevertheless, the Bible is the denomination's central source of doctrine. The CRC is Calvinistic, emphasizing the salvific power of God's grace through faith in Jesus Christ. Citing their belief in God's sovereignty over all areas of life, Christian Reformed theologians have highlighted the application of theology to current events and culture. This outward focus led the CRC to place a heavy emphasis on Christian education and service.

The importance of education and service within his home denomination informed Ehlers's entire life. At every stage of his schooling and development, he discovered ways to tie his love of academic studies to his desire to address real-world problems. Ehlers's pattern of service began with his parents, who had modeled hard work and faithfulness to their children. Ehlers was given opportunities to serve his community both through his church in Grand Rapids and through opportunities at Calvin College, an educational institution of the Christian Reformed Church, where he was a physics professor from 1966 to 1983. Ehlers's work at Calvin also nurtured his sense of what it can look like for members of the CRC to navigate politics. This intellectual and spiritual underpinning would guide and justify his decisions at every level of politics.

Childhood and College Years

In general, Ehlers didn't speak much about his childhood, but the modesty, work ethic, and Dutch frugality of his immigrant parents, John Willem Christian Ehlers and Alice Doorn Ehlers, were evident in his own life. John immigrated in 1912 with his mother and three younger siblings. They joined their father in Kalamazoo, who had left them four months earlier to find a place for the family to live.[6] The younger children attended John Street Christian School in Kalamazoo, where their classes were taught in Dutch. John enrolled in the Kalamazoo Public High School because he was determined to learn English as quickly as possible. John would remain a studious man; he attended Calvin Seminary and held ministerial posts in various Christian Reformed churches in the Midwest and Canada.[7]

The Doorns, Ehlers's mother's family, hailed from Bussum, not far away from Hilversum. Alice was the youngest of nine children, and her father died when she was only three years old. When she was eighteen years old, she emigrated with her sixty-five-year-old mother and older sister to join some of her older brothers, who had already settled in the US. The Doorn women traveled to Grand Rapids, Michigan, to reunite with other relatives. They attended Eastern Avenue Christian Reformed Church.

Alice and John were married on June 28, 1925, and they eventually were blessed with four children: Frances, Henrietta, Clarence, and Vernon. Vernon was born in Pipestone, Minnesota, near Edgerton, where his father was the minister of a small Christian Reformed church. John and Alice would move several times during their life together, finally retiring to Celeryville, Ohio.

Vern didn't have a strong sense of what he wanted to do when he grew up. He suffered from severe asthma for much of his childhood, which forced him to do his schooling at home. Ehlers tried to start the school year with his siblings several

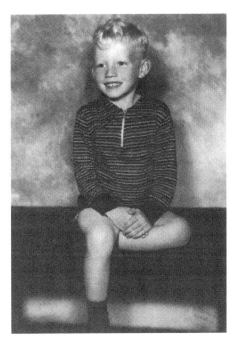

Ehlers, age four

times, but he never made it through the year. His older sister Fran brought home his assignments. His mother worried about her sickly son; sometimes his breathing was so strained that John and Alice feared he wouldn't reach adulthood. But young Vern did survive, and the time alone allowed him develop a lively life of the mind. He claimed Teddy Roosevelt as his childhood hero, because Roosevelt too had once been a boy with asthma. "In spite of many troubles, he [Roosevelt] managed to get a lot done," Ehlers later remarked to a reporter.[8]

It was as a child that Ehlers realized just how much there was to "get done" in the world. The solitary Ehlers became a voracious reader. "We couldn't believe it," said Ehlers's sister, Hennie, "but he taught himself to read, and he would read anything he put his hands on."[9] Like his father, he enjoyed studying. He read eight books a week and would have read more if the library hadn't set a limit of two books per card. (Ehlers short-circuited the system and used his siblings' library cards too). Ehlers showed an early interest in science, so his sister Fran bought him a subscription to *Popular Science*. A few years later, he graduated to *National Geographic*. Ehlers read every issue cover to cover. He devoured the news and often listened to the radio for updates during World War II. At a very young age, he started regularly zipping through *Time* magazine every week, a habit that continued for the next seventy years.

As Ehlers grew older and took on more responsibilities, he did not find a lot of time to expand the scope of his reading. He listed the Bible as his favorite book, and of course he kept up a steady diet of news.[10] Ehlers occasionally indulged in some fiction as well. He enjoyed C. S. Lewis's works and Tolkien's fantasy, and the physicist in him relished the sci-fi romp *Hitchhiker's Guide to the Galaxy*. He remained a lifelong supporter of his local library.

Ehlers believed his interest in politics started with the curiosity of his childhood. He said in an interview, "I think that experience made me particularly aware of the world around me. I think that had some effect on my consciousness of the world and what was necessary for good government."[11] While Alice always feared that her son was perhaps too much "in the world" with his political pursuits, John watched his son's career with pride.[12] Ehlers and his father were both mild-mannered men, with quiet and quirky senses of humor. In an interview, Ehlers's wife, Johanna (Jo), suggested that his patience in the face of criticism was also inherited from John Ehlers, who had learned to deal with criticism as a lifelong pastor.

In those days, Calvin College was the natural choice for any college-bound child of the CRC. Vern was extremely nervous when he arrived on campus because this was his first time actually *going to* school. He didn't know what he wanted to study, or if he was even good at academics at all. Vern was surprised when he scored high on the entrance exams. One Calvin professor happened to suggest that Vern might enjoy physics. So Vern stumbled into the discipline and, despite his worries, thrived at Calvin.

Rebels with a Ruminant:
Four Guys with a Goat

Ehlers's Calvin days were, for the most part, filled with long hours of study and typical college activities. However, he participated in one slightly notorious incident, which is here told by one of the coconspirators, Sam Bosch.

In the fall of 1954, Maurice [Mo Veenstra] enlisted Vern Ehlers, Frank Goertsema, and me into "doing something" with a goat he had acquired. Looking back on it, I don't know how Mo got Frank and Vern to also participate; they did not have the campus reputation that would lead you to believe they would be willing accomplices.

One late night shortly thereafter, we took the goat to Grace Hall, a women's dorm on Franklin Street, across from the Calvin library. I climbed up the fire escape to the third floor, carrying the goat over my shoulders, opened an unlocked door, and thrust the goat inside. We waited in the alley below.

Finally, the goat "licked" one of the gals' hands or face, which of course terrified her, and she let out a scream. Soon everyone on the third floor was screaming, which is what we had hoped for. Afterward, while I was driving down the narrow alley to pick up Mo, Vern, and Frank, a car came down the alley toward me. I quickly started to back up when another car came down the alley from behind—both vehicles were police cars. We told them we were not burglars, just some guys pulling off a college prank.

To ascertain whether we were really college students and not felons, the cops brought the four of us to the front of Grace Hall, which by this time was fully lit. All the residents were awake, including the house mother, Aunt Caroline. She told the police this was a college matter to be taken care of internally, and they did not have to report it as a crime. After thinking about it for a few minutes, the cops agreed.

▶

Sam Bosch, Vern, and
fellow goaters

The next morning, there was a notice on the bulletin board in the administration building demanding that the following students—Bosch, Ehlers, Gortsema, and Veenstra—report to Dr. Henry Decker, the ex-chemistry prof who was then in charge of campus discipline. Dr. Decker informed us that we four were to appear before a faculty discipline committee. The final verdict was that we were to be "campused" for two weeks, which meant that we could attend classes but do little else; we were expected not to leave our residences after 6:00 p.m.

Epilogue: In addition to being amateur scoundrels, the four goaters were also scholars. All earned graduate degrees, three of them PhDs.

~ Adapted from an account by Sam Bosch

Berkeley

In the 1950s, Calvin physics majors completed their undergraduate degrees at larger institutions. Ehlers transferred to the University of California, Berkeley, to finish his baccalaureate and stayed there to pursue graduate studies. He joined the research group of William Nierenberg, a physicist who had worked on the Manhattan Project. Nierenberg's team used a well-established "atomic beam method" to measure the magnetic properties and internal energies of various kinds of atoms. Their main innovation was to extend these techniques to make extremely precise measurements, even on atoms that were radioactively unstable. Their experiments were in fact so sensitive as to reveal differences between the behaviors of different isotopes of a single element. In other words, they were able to measure the magnetic effects of adding or subtracting a single neutron within

Original Caption: "Dr. Vernon J. Ehlers and Thomas Fowler operating the atomic beam magnetic-resonance apparatus at the University of California at Berkeley. Dr. Ehlers used the equipment last summer to measure the nuclear magnetic moment of Rb^{85}, and also to determine the atomic magnetic moment of Gallium."

the nucleus of an atom. For his dissertation, Vern focused on the specific case of gallium isotopes. The radioactive lifetime of one of these isotopes (Ga-70) was so short (twenty-one minutes) that his experiments called for a fast helicopter transport from the reactor where the sample was produced to the lab where the measurements were to be made. The pace of Vern's own progress seems to have been similarly rapid, as it was only four years between the conferral of his undergraduate degree and the submission date of his PhD thesis, "Nuclear Spins and Moments of Radioactive Gallium," in 1960.[13]

Outside the lab, Ehlers developed additional interests. He became friends with another Calvin physics transplant to Berkeley, Roger Griffioen, who was doing postdoctoral work and attended church with Ehlers. Griffioen would become one of Ehlers's closest colleagues and lifelong friends.

Mr. & Mrs. Ehlers, June 14, 1958

It was through another Calvin-Berkeley connection that Ehlers met a young woman, Johanna (Jo) Meulink from Ripon, California, about an hour outside of Berkeley. Yet another of Ehlers's Calvin friends at Berkeley was dating Johanna's roommate. One day, as the ladies were walking home from church, Ehlers and his friend rolled up in their car to say hello as they were coming into Ripon. Less than a week later, Ehlers had invited Jo to a Young Calvinist Convention. Jo, also a child of the Christian Reformed Church, accepted. When Jo met Ehlers, she was working as a secretary at a local Ripon doctor's office. Ehlers accepted an offer from a local family to stay with them when he visited. Soon, he was spending most of his weekends in Ripon. During his weekdays in the lab, the smitten physicist wrote letters to Jo. After about a year and a half, the two were engaged to be married. Their wedding was held in Ripon on June 14, 1958, and they moved immediately back to Berkeley, where Vern was still working on his dissertation.

From 1961 to 1962, the young Ehlerses moved to Germany, for a postdoc at the University of Heidelberg. They both loved to travel; this was the first of many international excursions that they would enjoy together. Their first child, Heidi, was born in Heidelberg four weeks before her adventurous parents were

The Ehlers family, 1972

scheduled to travel back to America via boat. "We had no money in those days," said Jo, "so we had to take the cheapest passage."[14] They squeezed their luggage and a "chintzy," second-hand baby buggy into a tiny cabin in one of the least desirable locations on the ship. Jo looks back on that exciting chapter of their life with affection; they made it back to Berkeley in one piece. Their next child, Brian, was born there, while Marla and Todd arrived after the family moved to Grand Rapids in 1966.

During the Berkeley years, Ehlers's interest in national news didn't flag. Among the papers, equations, rubrics, and files he saved from his student days are also numerous magazines and newspaper clippings about national events. The infamous student anti-Vietnam riots of 1966 occurred right under Vern and Jo's noses when they were living in Berkeley. Looking back, Vern believes this exposure would later influence his decision to go into politics. "I decided there were better ways of changing the course of government than taking to the streets, so I got involved in a party."[15]

In the early '60s, Vern and Jo didn't have any intention of moving their young family from California.[16] After all, they were deeply involved in their local church,

Walnut Creek CRC, where they had been founding members. Berkeley was a leading center in the field of physics, which was good for Ehlers's professional advancement. He had received offers from other institutions and declined them. But requests from his alma mater were difficult to ignore. Roger Griffioen, who had since moved back to work at Calvin, urged Ehlers to consider joining him. The Calvin physics department was young and full of potential. Plans for a new science building were in the works—this was just the kind of strategic, hands-on project that Ehlers loved. Finally, in 1965, Nierenberg left Berkeley for a new position as director of the Scripps Institution of Oceanography. With his former advisor gone, Ehlers sensed that it was a good time for change and, after much deliberation, accepted a position at Calvin.

It was in Grand Rapids that Ehlers would finally transition from watching politics to becoming a player himself. If the family had stayed in Berkeley, it is unlikely that Ehlers would have ever considered politics. Grand Rapids, a small city full of invested and engaged communities, was bursting with opportunities for political involvement.

Political Engagement at Eastern Avenue CRC and Calvin College

Ehlers got his first practice in political activism through his church in Grand Rapids. He and Jo knew a few families at Eastern Avenue CRC who made up a coterie of like-minded believers who also wanted to enact change. The urban church, contrary to the pull of white flight, decided to stay in the predominately black Baxter neighborhood on the city's southeast side. The church developed close ties to the black community in Grand Rapids and to this day remains committed to enacting social justice in its neighborhood.

As a congregant and later as an elder at Eastern Avenue CRC, Ehlers participated in numerous ministries. The church's focus on social justice showed Ehlers ways he could begin to combine his faith, sense of civic duty, and scientific expertise. Ehlers accepted a position on the 1976 CRC Synod's Task Force on World Hunger, a popular social conversation at the time. It was demanding work, but Ehlers enjoyed the project immensely.[17] Two books came out of the taskforce:

And He Had Compassion on Them (1978) and *For My Neighbor's Good* (1979), both of which Ehlers coauthored.

However, Ehlers's most influential experiences at Eastern Avenue CRC came through friendships that cultivated his social conscience and encouraged political activism. When Ehlers arrived in Grand Rapids in the '60s, he quickly became a key member of an unofficial group of local activists at Eastern Avenue CRC. Dennis and Jeni Hoekstra, in particular, became friends of Vern and Jo. The two couples, along with others in the church, were eager to find ways to improve the church's immediate neighborhood. They were also concerned with the racism within the city. The group worked for social change in two significant ways. First, they provided services to their neighborhood. Vern personally oversaw a committee that helped find funds to send neighborhood children to Christian schools. He and Jo contributed to the early development of Eastern Avenue CRC's housing outreach program, which eventually became the Inner City Christian Federation (ICCF). ICCF continues to help create and maintain affordable housing in Grand Rapids.[18] Ehlers shared his time and talents liberally. He recalled to an interviewer in 2010 how he and other Eastern Avenue CRC members would teach classes about insulation in houses and other home-care issues.

The Ehlerses, Hoekstras, and others in the group would strategize about who in the community might be good leaders. Then they approached these potential candidates and encouraged them to run for office; they even offered their services as campaign volunteers.[19] Working together, members from Eastern Avenue CRC and their neighbors were instrumental in getting the first wave of African American leadership elected in Grand Rapids.[20] Whether he knew it or not, assisting other candidates gave Ehlers the exposure to politics he would need when he ran for office himself. Through church work, Ehlers became aware of the issues, learned how to run a campaign, and practiced communicating effectively with the public.

Reformed Politics in Action

The 1960s and '70s were rich times for Christian Reformed engagement in politics in Grand Rapids. Calvin College students and faculty were no exception. At Calvin, President William Spoelhof's administration gave strong support to faculty members who wished to get involved in their community leadership. As an institution, Calvin saw those "endeavors as an extension of their Christian stewardship."[22] When Ehlers was elected to the county commission in 1974, he was one of seven faculty who held elected office. Steve Monsma and Paul Henry served in the state legislature; Harold Dekker (of Calvin Theological Seminary) and history professor Howard Rienstra were city commissioners; education professor Peter DeBoer sat on the Grand Rapids Board of Education; and mathematician Carl Sinke served as a Kentwood city commissioner.[23]

The "Calvin Crowd," as one newspaper article had dubbed them, spanned both sides of the aisle. However, unlike other outspokenly Christian politicians, these public servants did not get embittered in their ideological disagreements. Ehlers's fellow Calvin College colleague and friend City Commissioner Howard

Rienstra explained to a reporter in 1985, "There is a world and life view in Calvinism; that the responsibility of the Christian is not only to be saved out of this world, but to transform the world in the name of Christ."[24] The Calvin Crowd shared a Calvinistic view of the world's brokenness and the belief that all people bear God's image. The Christian Reformed tradition accepted government as a peaceful mechanism for creating a society in which all people are treated with equal dignity and can use their gifts. These fundamental beliefs transcended potential ideological differences.

The Calvin professor-politicians also did not view the political podium as a pulpit. Rienstra claimed that Reformed politicians tended to not "wear their religious beliefs on their political sleeves.[25] So, rather than attempting to win the system over to a "Christian" viewpoint on certain moral issues, the Calvin Crowd allowed their worldview to help them identify places where human dignity could be better served. They strove to model Christian virtue by maintaining high personal moral standards and encouraging life-giving policy, instead of spouting doctrine into the political arena. For Ehlers, this meant conducting politics with Micah 6:8 as his overarching set of principles: justice, mercy, and humility.

State Representative Paul Henry and Kent County Board of Commissioners Chairman Vernon Ehlers, from "The Calvin Connection: Making Room for Politics," *West Michigan Magazine,* December 1980.

Political scientist and Calvin professor Doug Koopman has called Ehlers's career a superb example of intellectual Reformed politics. Ehlers carried the principles of his childhood and Christian Reformed training into his scientific and political career with faithfulness and consistency. Part of the way Ehlers enacted faithfulness was by doing his homework. He believed that his intellect should be used for good, so he brought all of his wit and acumen to the complicated issues he studied, whether in the lab or in the legislature. If God is behind all of creation, then all of it should be understood and protected. This view of

God's sovereignty allowed Ehlers to pursue both of his careers as faithful expressions of his singular Micah 6:8 commitment.

In a speech titled "Enhancing and Protecting Life," Ehlers articulated a personal manifesto on how he logically applied his faith to real policy issues. He named four guiding principles that were particularly important in his professional life: justice, the sanctity of human life, God's sovereignty, and God's revelation to humanity, all of which align with the Reformed vision of public service. Ehlers's application of these principles to the problem of abortion demonstrates the distinct Christian Reformed pattern of his moral decision making. Like his fellow Republicans, Ehlers voted pro-life consistently. But his personal understanding of the abortion issue was far more nuanced and studied.

The Sanctity of Human Life: Ehlers on Abortion

Ehlers began his discussion on abortion by admitting his distaste for the underlying premise of the debate. He believed that the *Roe v. Wade* decision should have been left to state courts and that more time should have been allotted to thoroughly research the situation before dramatically polarizing the issue. The black-and-white nature of the pro-life/pro-choice debate frustrated Ehlers. He wrote, "The sloganeering ignores the many complexities that lie in the vast gray area between these two poles. The demagogic terminology virtually forces one to choose one polar view or the other."[26]

In the same speech, Ehlers compared the current binary landscape with past opinions from before *Roe v. Wade*. He noted that the church fathers, such as Calvin, Luther, and Augustine, don't have a consensus about when life begins. He drew extensively from a 1971 study conducted by a Christian Reformed Church task force that had been asked to survey pertinent information about abortion in the Bible. Ehlers noted that the members of the task force disagreed about the humanness of an embryo or fetus. Also, one member of the committee, Calvin Seminary professor Henry Stob, wrote that abortion could be considered for the following reasons: to save the mother's life, to prevent the birth of a "deformed or deranged" child, "to forestall dire personal and social consequences," and possibly "to preserve the physical and mental health of the mother." "Today," observed

Ehlers, "with the polarized views of abortion, it is unlikely that any Calvin Seminary professor could make such a statement and remain employed."

Ehlers noted that the either-or stance on abortion implies that the rights of the mother are in opposition to the rights of the child, which is not necessarily true. He acknowledged that medical advancements have changed the stage at which a fetus is viable, which also complicates the question of when life begins. When Ehlers answered questions from his constituents about abortion, he stated clearly that he was pro-life, but he was quick to nuance his opinion. He explained to a constituent in 1993 that, while he was certainly pro-life, he also supported pregnancy prevention.[27] He thought abortions should be considered when the mother's life is at risk.[28] In general, Ehlers tried to avoid the abortion topic altogether. He hoped to make truly beneficial progress in politics by focusing on other areas that were closer to his expertise.

Maintaining a safe distance from the abortion issue did not keep him from getting involved in other life-science policy areas. He worked extensively on anti–human cloning legislation, but he supported cloning experimentation on animals. While he had the utmost respect and confidence in scientific innovation (certainly more than the average legislator, given his academic training), following the Christian Reformed doctrine, Ehlers believed all life is sacred and all humans bear God's image. These two truths demand we put limits on what science and society are allowed to do.

Ehlers on the Issues

Ehlers's life-affirming principles determined his stances on social policy as well. In the tradition of a Rockefeller Republican, he subscribed to fiscally conservative policies but more idiosyncratic stances on social issues. For example, Ehlers was against euthanasia and the death penalty. He voted in favor of certain pro-gun measures, but he also was an ardent supporter of fair housing, better healthcare, and public television.

As might be expected when the political rubber hits the road, there are likely to be tensions and inconsistencies in any politician's record. Strictly according to his voting record, Ehlers does not stand out as particularly liberal on many social issues. His insistence on fiscal responsibility did not give him a high rating on certain human rights issues.

However, Ehlers's position as a member of Congress required that he balance the pressure from his party and constituents. He had to strategically play to his policy strengths, which he did with success. He worked tirelessly on environmental reform and on increased funding for education. He always tried to preserve funding for preexisting government services. Equality issues weren't at the forefront of his policy areas, yet they were on his mind. "He really had a heart for social justice," explained Rick Treur, his district manager. "Concerns for the poor, making sure people had good health care—I think those stemmed from his religious background."[29] Ehlers cut his teeth on social-justice issues in his early days in Grand Rapids. His work at Eastern Avenue CRC exposed him to the racial injustice within his own community. Being a member of the CRC's task force on hunger sparked an interest in public health. All of these concerns stayed with him throughout his career.

Concerned as he was about equality, Ehlers was also willing to admit his personal prejudices and biases. He was an early supporter of women in leadership. In an interview, Ehlers reflected on his initial shock at the blatant gender inequality and sexism he saw in the county commission. Back then, the commission was very much, as Ehlers put it, "the good old boys club . . . and literally with the emphasis on boys. There was not a single woman in twenty-one people." Ehlers responded to the situation by trying to recruit more women.[30]

Ehlers's Micah 6:8 view of the world compelled him to keep examining his own motivations and prejudices about race as well. He realized that a just and equal society can only occur when people are honest with themselves. In his commencement speech to the class of 1998 at Michigan State University, Ehlers addressed his struggles with prejudice.

> For years I, as did most everyone I know, denied that I was racist, sexist, etc. . . . Yet when I began analyzing the problems of prejudice and discrimination in our world and what can be done about them, I began by searching deep in my soul, and realized that indeed I was a racist. . . .
> I have become convinced that we cannot solve issues of prejudice without each taking this first step of honest self-reflection. Thus I ask each of you to look deep into your hearts and minds, identify your prejudices of all sorts, and consciously work to eliminate them from your lives.[31]

It's difficult to imagine many politicians admitting as much today, but being honest about these issues was a way Ehlers "walked humbly." Throughout his career, Ehlers advocated for the inclusion of women and minorities in politics and the sciences. He was troubled by the lack of minorities in these fields, which need a multiplicity of voices in order to thrive.[32]

Christian principles learned in childhood were Ehlers's guide as he pursued his vocation. He worked hard to develop his scientific talents, and then he used that training to promote the flourishing of his community. His love of learning and solving problems could have taken him anywhere, but ultimately they found good soil and bore good fruit in a life of public service.

CHAPTER TWO
"Here's one hour's worth of ideas": Getting into Politics

Ehlers was excited to begin strategizing in his new position for the emerging science division at Calvin College. Soon after he accepted the position, he wrote a letter to department chair Roger Griffioen with thirty-five typed and numbered suggestions for the new science building, ranging from the plumbing to desks to usable space. Ehlers ended with the following astounding statement (when held against the length of the letter):

> Well, this is one hour's worth of ideas. I hope I will be able to
> come up with a few additional things, but I think this covers all
> the major points.[33]

Calvin gave Ehlers numerous opportunities to hone his strategizing and problem-solving skills. Eventually, he would take these skills and, based on his Micah 6:8 foundation, transition out of the academy and into politics.

"Full of Ideas—Full of Suggestions"

Many Calvin faculty members recollect Ehlers's drive to "fix" things around campus. He was "full of ideas—full of suggestions,"[34] recalled Roger Griffioen, who, besides being a close friend of Ehlers, also worked closely with him as a colleague in physics; each of them chaired the department at some point. Ehlers arrived at Calvin from Berkeley brimming with ideas about how to run things on campus. He approached every problem meticulously. For example, whenever the department needed to purchase new equipment, Griffioen would peruse some catalogs and make a relatively quick decision, whereas Ehlers researched *all* the different product options they had to choose from. "In the end we would usually have the same opinion," said Griffioen.

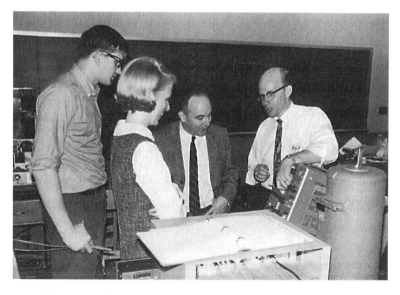

Ehlers with physics students at Calvin, late '60s / early '70s

While Ehlers's suggestions were often helpful, they could also be excessive. He wrote memos to the department chair, the dean, building services, or even the college president about the most mundane problems: a trash problem in the science building, inconvenient drain pipes on campus, a campaign for more aesthetically pleasing waste cans on campus, concerns about the curriculum, or new programming about current events. He also kept copies of many of these memos. Perhaps it was an inbred frugalness, but Ehlers was a consummate "saver," as Griffioen put it. He recalled finding Ehlers on campus on a Saturday morning after he had left for state politics. "He was cleaning things out. He had big canvas janitor carts—several of them—a couple already filled." Griffioen asked Ehlers whether he saved *everything*, to which Ehlers replied, "No, my offices would be filled floor to ceiling if I saved everything. I had to learn not to!"[35] Ehlers relished the process of doing homework and documenting his work. His meticulous and logical methods meant that he kept thorough records of what he accomplished.

Given his tendencies, the young physics professor readily took on work related to administration and strategic planning for the college. "It's really kind of odd when you think about [it]," recalled Ehlers's old friend and fellow Eastern Avenue CRC member Dennis Hoekstra: "In the same person was this interest and skill in mid-range strategy, and, at the same time, enough energy and interest to do that detail stuff."[36]

Ehlers was diplomatic in the way he approached people with his suggestions, but he did his utmost to get placed on important committees. He became something of a committee junkie and was often seen carrying two briefcases on campus: one for the courses he was teaching and one for his administrative work.

Perhaps his most important administrative contribution at Calvin was his work on the powerful Faculty Organization Study Committee, or FOSCO. One problem in those days involved faculty governance, specifically, the question of how decision-making power should be distributed across academic departments and faculty committees. Even though he was a relatively young faculty member, Ehlers convinced President Spoelhof that faculty organization needed special attention and that he could lead the effort. As chair of FOSCO, Ehlers gave shape to an administrative structure that survives at Calvin even today.[37]

Ehlers's puritan work ethic was formidable. Even as a young professor, he was a workaholic, regularly putting in eighty-hour weeks. He had an overwhelming sense of responsibility to use his gifts to do the most good, which he did cheerfully and faithfully. However, another side of his overriding sense of responsibility could also be characterized as meddling or a dangerous pattern of needing to be needed. This sense was evident even when he first accepted the position at Calvin. He wrote to President Spoelhof on November 4, 1965:

> This realization has been dawning on me throughout the
> months of discussion, but it was only upon reviewing all the
> material that it hit me with its full impact. The correspondence
> . . . made me poignantly aware of the tremendous need Calvin
> College has, not just for another physicist, but for me.[38]

Ehlers liked to be needed. He enjoyed being the possessor of all the facts and knowing, beyond a shadow of a doubt, that he was the best man for the job. And he understood his scientific training as a powerful springboard into administrative work of all kinds. He ran for the county commission because he had observed Kent County's solid waste problem. His friends encouraged him, telling him, "You're a scientist. You're the right guy for the job."[39] Ehlers would use his scientific credentials to justify the necessity of his presence at every level of government in which he served. Like any human being, Ehlers's motivations were mixed, but this should not diminish his truly remarkable contributions from his long hours of quiet effort.

Despite the delight he took in testing the limits of his own omnicompetence, the long hours took a toll. Ehlers wanted to spend more time at home—to help his kids with their homework and do projects around the house. He was often an absent father, which was difficult for him and his family. But Jo and the kids were supportive. Vern always called when he was going to be late, and the family grew accustomed to eating together much later in the evening than other families. As he got more involved with politics, the Ehlers kids would leave him notes on his briefcase and look forward to spending time with him on the weekends.

A letter from the Calvin days, written to Roger Griffioen, reveals Ehlers's awareness of his own tendency to take on an overloaded work schedule. The letter, entitled "Time or Lack Thereof," includes an itemized time budget for his weekly activities: advising, teaching, departmental duties, and a staggering nineteen-and-a-half hours of committee work. This list does not include the prep time he spent on his courses. In a tongue-in-cheek moment, Ehlers confided in Griffioen,

> I don't know why I am telling you all this, because there is not
> much you can do for me besides offer me a shoulder to cry on.
> Perhaps that's all I need. At any rate I would appreciate it if you
> would keep this in mind whenever any departmental duties are
> to be handed out. Also, if you ever catch me volunteering for
> another job or committee assignment, please shoot me.[40]

As time would tell, this self-awareness never gave way to self-restraint, and, as his daughter Marla said, "He never learned to say 'no.'"[41]

Ehlers saw the potential to do good in so many places. Unlike most physicists, he didn't pour all his efforts into one concentrated research subject. In good liberal arts fashion, his energies were far-flung. Griffioen found Ehlers's desire to fix a variety of problems inspiring. "That attitude has rubbed off on me," explained Griffioen.[42]

Ehlers's interest in public service was first sparked at the interface of science and policy. He saw the terrain of science-and-society issues as a place where he could find vocational fulfillment. Science advisory committees and solid waste disposal may seem unglamorous areas to most citizens, but for Ehlers they were the perfect place to start.

First Steps toward Politics: Science, Vern Ehlers, and Gerald R. Ford

Ehlers himself pinpointed the exact moment he cemented his interest in public policy to an American Physical Society (APS) meeting in 1972.[43] The Ehlers family spent the 1971–72 academic year in Boulder, Colorado, after Ehlers had been awarded a fellowship from the National Science Foundation to work at the Joint Institute for Laboratory Astrophysics on "an electron-atom scattering experiment and on a study of laser saturation of atomic transitions."[44] It was no doubt an intense year, but it was also the year that Ehlers caught the public service bug. In 1972, he attended a lecture by research-chemist-turned-congressman Mike McCormack (D-WA)[45] at an APS meeting in San Francisco. McCormack encouraged the physicists in the audience to write their representatives about scientific concerns. He wanted them to get involved, as scientists, in politics. The advice resonated with Ehlers's interests. He sent a letter to Gerald Ford, then our U.S. congressman representing Grand Rapids, offering to create and chair a science committee for his office. Ehlers did not anticipate a quick or positive response, but he received a phone call two days later from Ford's chief of staff. Ford loved the idea and wanted the committee to begin work soon.

Ehlers assembled a group of local scientists, both Democrats and Republicans: Carl Bajema (biology, Grand Valley State College). Edwin Krug (engineering, Lear-Siegler), Gordon Van Harn (biology, Calvin), John Van Zytveld (physics, Calvin), and Ehlers himself.[46] Ehlers's committee advised Ford until he became vice president, meeting once per quarter, about six meetings in all.[47]

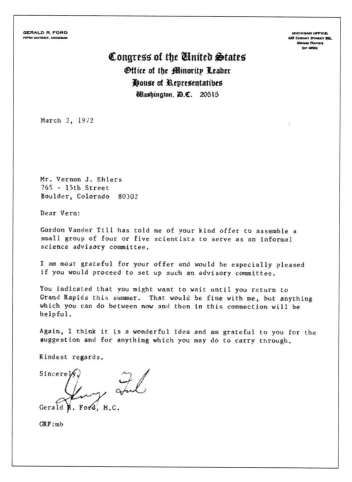

Letter from Gerald R. Ford to Vernon Ehlers about forming
a science advisory committee, March 2, 1972

In the Tradition of Jerry Ford, Paul Henry, and Vern Ehlers

Ehlers reaped highly practical benefits from his connection to Ford, whose beneficent persona still looms large in West Michigan. Ehlers was eager to draw connections between himself and Ford. Like Ford, Ehlers espoused a thoughtful and steady brand of leadership. Most importantly, all of the succeeding congressmen in Jerry Ford's seat have offered excellent constituency services, a tradition Ford set in motion. Many West Michiganders speak about their brand of representative with the phrase, "In the tradition of Jerry Ford, Paul Henry, and Vern Ehlers."

In their science advisory meetings, Ehlers was impressed with Ford's curiosity and willingness to ask good questions.[48] Ehlers personally admired Ford's ability to remember people's names and interact with the people he represented, a skill Ehlers tried to emulate. He took any comparison made between himself and Ford as the highest compliment. Ford and Ehlers remained friendly throughout Ford's life. When Ehlers won his congressional bid, Ford called him to congratulate him personally. Ehlers was instrumental in awarding the Congressional Gold Medal, one of the highest civilian honors, to Jerry and Betty Ford in 1998.

Sprucing Up Kent County: First Campaign

Ehlers ran for the county commission in 1974 as a relatively unknown candidate. But his connections to Ford, the experience he had through politicking with his fellow Eastern Avenue CRC members, and his committee work at Calvin had equipped him with more than enough experience to be a good commissioner. Ehlers had tried to run for an elected position on the Grand Rapids City Charter Committee the previous year and lost, and there was no guarantee that he would win the county commissioner position either.

The campaign highlighted his capability. The slogan read loud and proud: "A candidate who understands the issues and takes a stand." Ehlers's main issues were environmental standards, better management of the county jail, revenue sharing, and solid waste disposal. Ehlers boosted his name recognition with his "Spruce up Kent County" slogan and his distribution of spruce seedlings. Jo, the four Ehlers kids, and an army of volunteers assembled the seedlings and distributed them. In these early days, he campaigned from the living room—a low-budget headquarters. The Ehlers family and their friends from Calvin College and Eastern Avenue CRC pitched in helping with food, stuffing envelopes, answering calls, and running errands. The campaign relied on high numbers of volunteers to keep costs down (one opposing candidate outspent Vern three to one).[49] Still, the margin of the race was, as Ehlers put it, "excruciatingly close."[50] He won the 1974 primary by a mere 118 votes, and from then on, he never lost an election.[51]

Ehlers served four terms on the county commission, from 1975 to 1983, and was chair for three years. Those were long days. Ehlers was still a full-time professor, so the commission and other board meetings gobbled up any spare time. It wasn't unusual for Ehlers to start the day with a 7:00 breakfast meeting and end the day with yet more board meetings that dragged until 11:00 p.m. or midnight.[52]

In his rookie year on the county commission, Ehlers became the first freshman to serve on the personnel committee, the jail committee, and the subcommittee on solid waste. These also happened to be unpopular posts among the other commissioners.[53] Later, Ehlers was on the finance committee, was chair of the Board of Public Works, and was a member on the library board. Constituents appreciated Ehlers's leadership as chair because he was able to maintain the

Vern and volunteers celebrate his first victory, Kent County
Commission primary, 1974.

county's social services and balance the budget during the recession years of the early '80s.[54] His reputation for fiscal responsibility and conservative practices would be key as he ran for higher offices.

However, Ehlers's greatest legacy in the county commission was his solid-waste disposal and recycling initiatives in Kent County. In 1975, the county was scrambling to find a replacement for the Kentwood landfill, which was nearing its maximum capacity. Ehlers joined the team that investigated alternatives. He was on the commission when the Plainfield landfill was built on Ten Mile Road in Grand Rapids (this was later replaced by a recycling center).

Ehlers was instrumental in envisioning and acquiring grants for the Kent/Ottawa Resource Reuse Center on Market Street in downtown Grand Rapids. He was adamant that Kent County had to take recycling seriously if the future residents of the county were to enjoy a healthy standard of living, but generating momentum for recycling in Kent County required much negotiation and homework. There were tensions between the City of Grand Rapids, which wanted to implement recycling infrastructure as soon as possible, and the county Board of Public Works, which felt impelled to figure out how to dispose of solid waste responsibly before diving

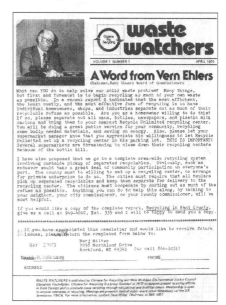

A newsletter from Vern supporting recycling efforts in Kent County

into recycling.[55] The timelines just didn't match up. Many long meetings followed, some of them acrimonious. However, Ehlers managed to secure a grant that enabled the county to build the Resource Reuse Center.

Ehlers wasn't even on the commission by the time many of his initiatives were put into place—the wheels of policy have always turned slowly. However, even as he moved into higher offices, Ehlers didn't lose interest in his local, hometown environmental projects. Beth Bandstra-Dekker, one of Ehlers's earliest campaign managers and later one of his staffers, ran for county commission herself when Ehlers moved to the Michigan state House. Ehlers pulled her aside after church one Sunday—they both attended Eastern Avenue CRC—and asked her specifically to keep up the work on the waste plant. "I knew nothing about waste management," recalled Bandstra-Dekker. But Ehlers, a true environmentalist even on Sunday morning, gave her a quick lesson. "I had to do my own homework," said Beth, "but, as it happens, I managed to get those twenty other commissioners to go for it, and now we have a great plant in western Michigan. Had he not said that to me, I'm not sure I would have gotten on the track to learn about it. . . . I give him the credit."[56] Ehlers's legacy as a commissioner lives on in the tangible recycling infrastructure he helped implement. By the time he left the commission, the Kent/Ottawa recycling program was the most comprehensive in the state.[57]

From County to State

As a county commissioner, Ehlers enjoyed the best of both worlds: he was enmeshed in local governance, *and* he could keep teaching and studying physics. But in 1982, Ehlers was faced with a decision that would define the rest of his professional life. Paul Henry had won the bid for West Michigan's state Senate seat, leaving his place in the Michigan state House open. Ehlers, with his close connections within the Michigan Republican Committee and his commissioner experience, was a favorite candidate. But pursuing state politics could also terminate his academic career. He would no longer have time to teach, research, or invest in campus life—activities that had defined him up to this point. New leadership opportunities would also put another strain on the Ehlers's home life: more meetings, more commuting, more time away from home. Ehlers struggled over the decision. But when he finally committed to politics, he slid naturally into his new profession. After all, he had been practicing political involvement for a long time. Henry's endorsement was more than generous:

> He has been an outstanding county commissioner and
> chairman of the county board. He's the ablest candidate the
> Republicans could have recruited in that district. I'm just
> happy we were able to convince him to run. There's no doubt
> in my mind that he will be an excellent legislator.[58]

Sure enough, Ehlers's campaign was successful. In the state House, he pursued issues that had sparked his interest in the county commission. In looking back at his entire political career, Ehlers highlighted his accomplishments in state legislature as some of his proudest moments. He often cited his hard-fought 911 expansion bill from 1984. At that time, only half of the states had 911 service. Ehlers had been interested in obtaining the service as a commissioner, and he promised final implementation in his state representative campaign. However, even at this level of government, it was difficult legislation. Everyone thought it was a good idea, but only Ehlers was willing to put in the decade of work to get the program off the ground.[59]

Ehlers in State House ca. 1983–85

Ehlers won his reelection campaign in 1984, but when his district's state Senate seat opened in the same year, he was faced with another decision: should he stay in the House or engage in yet another campaign for the Senate?

The State Senate Special Election of 1985

Most of Ehlers's campaigns were unremarkable for the simple reason that he won them so easily. However, the special election of 1985 for Michigan state Senate 32nd seat stands out for several reasons. It was a game of political musical chairs among three highly qualified, closely connected Christian Reformed politicians.[60] A quick overview of the race gives a good example of how Ehlers campaigned and how motivated and qualified candidates can raise the level of policy debate.

Paul Henry, a Republican, left the 32nd seat in the Michigan Senate vacant after he was elected to serve in the United States Congress. The same state Senate seat had also been held by Democrat Stephen Monsma, yet another former Calvin political science professor. Monsma had left the seat three years previously when he ran, unsuccessfully, for the "Jerry Ford seat" that Paul Henry (and Ehlers) eventually would win. Monsma ran to recapture the state Senate seat for the Democratic Party, while Ehlers rose through the primaries as the favored Republican candidate.

The voters of the 32nd district faced a dilemma difficult to imagine today. Two experienced candidates, who not only cited similarly fair-minded and moral motivations for their involvement in politics, but also were both sons of Dutch immigrants, members of the Christian Reformed Church, and professors at the same school. Monsma had

Artist's depiction of the choice voters faced between Ehlers and Monsma in the 1985 State Senate race.

served four years in the Michigan House and four in the Senate. Ehlers had spent only two years as state representative but eight years on the county commission.

This was the most expensive Michigan Senate race to date,[61] and both parties had high stakes in the outcome. Republicans had gained control of the Senate in 1983 and were eager to keep it. If a Democrat won the special election, the parties would be equally split with nineteen seats each. The lieutenant governor, a Democrat, would break tie votes. Nationally, the race was one of many attempts by Republicans to focus their energies on gaining majorities in local elections. A Washington Post article described the race as "tinged with racial overtones,"[62] as a Republican loss would shift power to senior Democrats on the east side of the state, which included Detroit's majority-black constituencies. Democrats had high hopes for Monsma, despite the usual Republican majority in the district. Monsma's previous experience in the Michigan Senate would earn him a spot on the powerful Appropriations Committee, thereby increasing the influence of his constituency. Ehlers could highlight his own experience but argued he could guarantee a balanced approach to state finances, unlike a more liberal candidate, and he could continue to work on environmental and education policy. In the letter he sent out announcing his candidacy, Ehlers claims the party believed he was "the only candidate who could hold this seat against strong [D]emocratic challenge."[63]

The campaign was grueling. Ehlers had only just finished securing his reelection to the House and was now forced to start yet another campaign. There were many opportunities to run a particularly nasty campaign, considering the close connections between the candidates. The Republican party attempted to smear Monsma's record in a letter sent out to party members, but Ehlers distanced himself from the letter and vowed that his office at least would run only clean and positive campaigns. As a general rule, Ehlers avoided even saying his opponent's name in order to focus all his rhetoric and energy on issues.

In a letter to a constituent, Ehlers explained that neither he nor Monsma was "particularly concerned" about running against the other.[64] They understood the political process, and each felt called to be involved. "I hope as we campaign against each other that it can be a good experience and we can demonstrate how Christians can run campaigns—on issues rather than distortions," explained Monsma in the Banner, the Christian Reformed Church's periodical.[65] In the same article, both men stressed the importance of doing justice. Ehlers said, "Being Christian politicians means that we are concerned with achieving justice for all." Monsma concurred, explaining that he approached policy issues with the question "What is 'just' here?"[66] From a political standpoint, it wasn't their differences that posed the biggest difficulties in their campaigns. It was their similarities. Both were moderates—Monsma was more conservative on certain local issues than his liberal colleagues, and Ehlers often had far more sympathy for liberal issues than other conservatives. Both brought an extremely high level of knowledge and competence to the table. One reporter called their debates "decidedly highbrow."[67] True to their professorial pasts, they were quick to point out the complexity of the policies under discussion. However, in the end, the balance and traditional stance that Ehlers espoused won the district. Ehlers carried the day with a 55% to 45% victory.

This particular race highlights certain traits that defined Ehlers as he rose in power. He reached across the aisle with respect and a genuine eagerness to get things done. The race serves a general reminder that two qualified and passionate people can want the same, good things, even if their methods and ideologies are opposed.

Ehlers served on the Natural Resources and Environmental Affairs, Health and Mental Health, Education, and Energy Committees in the Michigan Senate. He chaired Natural Resources and Environmental Affairs and was the vice chair for the Mental Health Committee later in his tenure. He spent the last six years of his time in the Senate as president pro tempore.

Ehlers fondly remembered these busy days in the state legislature. He loved sifting through the meticulous details of his technical committees, and he routinely

Ehlers presiding in newly restored Michigan Senate chamber, January 1990.

Public Act 14 of 1987

One of Ehlers's most important Michigan Senate contributions was his sponsorship of Public Act 14 of 1987. The bill expanded state-mandated screenings of newborns. In 2015, the Michigan Newborn Screening initiative celebrated its fifty-year anniversary. Ehlers played an important role in this public health story. The fiftieth-anniversary informational book explains,

> In 1987, Senator Ehlers, with help from Dr. Allen and Dr. Charles Whitten, introduced and guided a groundbreaking bill through the legislative process. Public Act 14 of 1987 doubled the screening panel from three to six disorders, adding Biotinidase Deficiency (BIOT), Maple Syrup Urine Disease (MSUD) and Sickle Cell Disease (SCD). The legislation also established a fee for each filter paper test card sold, assuring a more stable funding source to cover the costs associated with laboratory testing and follow-up. Senator Ehlers would remain a strong advocate for newborn screening both as a state Senator and later as a member of the U.S. Congress from Michigan's 3rd congressional district.[68]

This bill paved the way for more progress to be made for infant health and saved thousands of babies' lives. Ehlers was particularly proud of his part on this legislation. He told a reporter many years later that this kind of legislation is not only good policy but Christian work.[69] Better health raises the standard of living for all society.

passed more bills than his colleagues. However, there were always pressures. Ehlers never enjoyed great health; his asthma sometimes acted up, and he continued to spend a lot of time away from home. He commuted to Lansing almost daily when the House and Senate were in session. Heaven forbid he should miss a vote. But Ehlers was as frugal with his time as he was with money. He used the commuting time to dictate letters or notes on a recording device as he drove. Even while multitasking, his command of details is impressive. On the tapes, his mid-range baritone plods on evenly, with very few mistakes or stops. He verbally included his punctuation so his secretary would be in no doubt of what he wanted typed up later.

Ehlers's dedication did not go unnoticed. When Ehlers left the Senate in 1993, some of his colleagues on the Natural Resources Committee issued a special tribute to him. Part extended thank-you note and part gentle joke, the tribute highlights just what made Ehlers such an effective, and quirky, state legislator.[70] Affectionately dubbing him "the indoor-outdoorsman," the committee thanks Ehlers for teaching them that "recycling makes cents" and for his unending drive to improve Michigan's natural resources down to the smallest, grimy detail (the cleanliness of park toilets included). Ehlers's meticulous attention to details may have seemed overbearing at times, but his presence in the Senate pushed his colleagues to pass thorough policy, and they appreciated it. They also appreciated his peculiar sense of humor and were perfectly ready to dish a bit of it back at him, as evidenced in their list of Ehlers's legacies.

- Cleaner Parks. As chair of the Senate Natural Resources Appropriations Subcommittee, the State went $70 million in debt and sold the Accident Fund to assure that no human scat would ever again be found in State Parks showers. A clean restroom is worth it.
- Cleaner Gas Stations. While chair of the Senate Natural Resources and Environmental Affairs Committee, he immersed himself in LUST issues, and created the MUSTFA fund to help clean things up...even though "7/8 cents was never enough".
- Cleaner Laws. With painstaking attention to detail, he continuously introduced technical legislation to correct grammar and syntax, and to recodify all environmental laws for easy reading by the general public.
- Wiser Resource Use. His personal philosophy, and his State recycling law, taught us that recycling makes cents. We admire his re-use of 1965 Christmas wrap this year and the mouse habitats created from his 200+ boxes stored in the Records Center. For his few items of discard, he taught us the "Dutch Stomp" (not to be confused with the dance).
- More Fun Places. Under the Senator's tutelage, over 425 local recreation opportunities have been funded, including ball parks, ice arenas, and yes, better public restrooms; and

Section of State of Michigan Special Tribute, December 22, 1993

Ehlers brought all of himself to the job—his work ethic, his skills with details, his strategic abilities. He also brought integrity and kindness. These attributes won him respect and goodwill from his colleagues. However, new challenges were ahead: difficult transitions, new gridlock, and higher stakes. He would soon have to answer yet another political calling, this time to Washington.

CHAPTER THREE

Mr. Ehlers Goes to Washington: Challenges in Congress

Ehlers never lost his academic taste for study, discussion, and problem solving. He found similarities between Congress and the academic life, claiming Congress sometimes felt like "one big faculty meeting."[71] However, the transition from state legislature to Congress highlighted one of the most difficult and frustrating elements of politics for Ehlers. At the national level, Ehlers discovered that policy moved much more slowly than it had back in Lansing. There was also less time for thoughtful discussion and, much to Ehlers's chagrin, illogical decision making ran rampant on the Hill. Ehlers was quoted in a *Washington Post* article:

> Vern Ehlers says Gingrich's idea to give every child a laptop
> computer would have launched an interesting give-and-take
> on campus, but in Washington it turned into headlines without
> debate on the proposal's merits. "It's one of the hard lessons
> of politics that you can't just throw out ideas for discussion like
> in academia. It can be stifling."[72]

Ehlers missed the valuing of complexity, debate, and problem solving he enjoyed in academia and in county and state politics, and even in his race against Steve Monsma. Ehlers's nitty-gritty, highly detailed approach to policy did not work as easily in a body of four hundred people. Unlike more traditional politicians,

Ehlers was not a speechifying visionary. He was personally unable to rally his colleagues through rhetoric, back slapping, and socializing. He could offer anecdotes, but he didn't pursue sound bites. A go-getting mentality came naturally to Ehlers, but he continually had to work on crafting more compelling speeches. He preferred the technical legislation and the problems that could be solved through hard work, logical deductions, and good principles. However, at a congressional level of governance, not all decisions can be made through hard work and logic. And Ehlers was faced with some decisions that defied his Micah 6:8 principles.

A Conflicted Call to Congress

Paul Henry died of brain cancer at the age of 51, soon after he had been elected for his fourth term in Congress. He had been diagnosed nine months previously, and his health steadily declined. He rallied enough to attend his swearing-in ceremony but died soon after. After Henry's diagnosis, Ehlers's friends and the Republican leadership encouraged him to run for the seat. But Ehlers was extremely uncomfortable with the proposition. Although he certainly had thought of running, he was extremely sensitive to Henry's family and staff. He had no desire to make a predatory political move before anyone knew Paul's prognosis. There was also the question of whether he wanted to seek higher office at all. Ehlers was president *pro tem* in the state Senate and waist deep in a slew of important legislation. The work was satisfying and not too far from home. Running for Congress would disrupt life as the Ehlers family knew it. "Oh, that was a very difficult time," recalled Jo, "but Providence helped us there too."[73]

Shortly before Paul Henry's death, Vern and Jo were scheduled to attend a conference in San Diego. People were pressuring Vern to announce his bid for the seat, but, as Jo said, "he didn't know what to do, and I didn't know what to say either. He had to have the feeling in his own heart."[74] So the Ehlers family went on their "vacation" with the hopes that being away would give them some sense of clarity.

During the conference, Ehlers attended a Sunday morning service, where the chaplain delivered a mediation on, of all things, "going where you are called." It was exactly what he needed to hear. In a conversation with his daughter Marla, Vern explained how the experience aided his decision making. When the Ehlerses returned from San Diego, he consulted with Henry's staff and his wife, Karen. With their blessing, he announced his bid for the seat.

On December 8, 1993, the votes were tallied, and Ehlers was easily elected to fill Henry's seat, by 67% of the vote, beating two other candidates: Democrat Dale Sprik and independent Dawn Krupp.[75] The primary had been a closer call,

Vern and Jo celebrate the news of congressional victory, 1993

since nine Republicans ran for the seat.[76] But Ehlers's contingent of volunteers (about 950 all together) ran an old-school campaign. Aside from a thirty-second TV ad, they stuck to the basics: canvassing neighborhoods and making time for individual encounters.[77]

Events in December 1993 moved toward Ehlers's Christmas break at a wild pace. Because this was a special election, Ehlers was immediately placed on the congressional payroll after his victory. But he still had responsibilities in the Michigan Senate. A new education budget was up for a vote, and the state Republicans were eager to have him back in Lansing. At the same time, Ehlers was trying to get acquainted with Henry's staff, who were heroically holding down the fort in Washington, and to figure out his new congressional responsibilities. "That Christmas," recalled Marla, "The senate went into a session on December 23rd and they didn't wrap up until the 24th. That was a crazy transition."[78] A few weeks later, in January 1994, Ehlers assumed his congressional duties.

Team Gingrich

Ehlers joined the United States 103rd Congress on the eve of Newt Gingrich's speakership and the "Republican Revolution" of 1994. It was an auspicious moment for someone of Vern's skills and experience. Ehlers was eager to gain the respect of his colleagues. He told *American Physical Society News* in 1994, "In the political world, the amount you can get accomplished is directly proportional to the degree of respect that your colleagues have for you. And so I'm working on that so my new colleagues will trust my judgement on some of the issues."[79] The insatiably curious Ehlers learned during his first year in office that he could not be an expert in everything; he had to specialize in his particular skills in order to establish credibility.[80] Fortunately, Ehlers's skills and experience brought him to Gingrich's attention. Ehlers had participated in a switch to a Republican majority in Michigan. So, Gingrich asked Ehlers to share a pep talk of sorts with Republican representatives.[81] The result was a six-page article, "Up in Michigan: Lessons for Becoming a Majority," later published in the *Catalyst* magazine.

Ehlers takes part in a mock swearing-in ceremony with House Speaker Newt Gingrich, January 7, 1997. Inscription: "To Vern Congratulations—thank you for all your help, your friend Newt."

The letter provides insight into Ehlers's conception of Republicanism in the early '90s. Ehlers begins with his own experience as a state Republican. He addresses the defeatist minority mentality he saw in the 103rd Congress. If the party wanted to be the majority, it needed to act like it would win. Ehlers argued that momentum for victory flows from a cohesive agenda, which was lacking in the party. In order to have an agenda, individual members must be willing to make compromises. Ehlers summed it up simply:

If the GOP really wants to achieve the majority, everyone is
going to have to learn to set aside a good deal of their own
agenda and buy into a unified group agenda.[82]

Ehlers recognized the need for good leadership to rally an anemic minority
into a vibrant, goal-driven majority; he referenced John Engler's leadership in
Michigan and Gingrich's potential to be a great rallier of the troops in Congress.

"Up in Michigan" ended with several prescient statements about "issues"
the party needed to address. True to form, Ehlers insisted the party must focus on
issues and not ideology, and the issues should not be specific. The article explic-
itly addressed abortion; if the party continued to define itself based on specific
issues like "pro-life vs. pro-choice," it could lose key votes. Finally, Ehlers also
pinpointed the party's Achilles heel:

We really have to work once again to attract the minority vote,
with minority candidate recruitment as a key part of that effort
and an emphasis on our compassion. We must change our
image from being the "hard-nosed" people and convey the
fact that we are seriously interested in dealing with people's
problems. Then we must use our image as policy makers and
people who can govern to show that we have solutions that
really work, that address the root of the problem.[83]

Ehlers's underlying Micah 6:8 desire to serve people with practical governance comes through in his statement. But the words may also seem quaint in ret-
rospect. The Republican party did not progress along the lines Ehlers suggested.
The party continued to splinter due to its inability to focus on issues, and the internal gridlock contributed to even greater gridlock between the two parties. The
Gingrich years were another chapter in the story of the increasingly divisive partisanship we see in legislation today. Likewise, the use of polarizing language has
stymied progress. Ehlers saw government as a way to solve problems, a principle
that some politicians seem to relinquish.

Ehlers never agreed with all of Gingrich's ideology. However, in those early
days, Ehlers was impressed by Gingrich's charisma. Like Ehlers himself, Gingrich
had been a professor and could explain complex issues clearly. However,
Gingrich had the added gift of charm and persuasion. The combination made

him a powerful force for change, which Ehlers recognized and applauded. He was willing to defend Gingrich despite their ideological differences.

Portrait commissioned in honor of Vern's committee chairmanship, 2006

The Republican Party did win a majority fifty-four seats in the 104th Congress. During the preceding year, Ehlers had established enough credibility with party leadership to be given a role, if a only a small one, on the nicknamed "Team Gingrich," the group of House members enlisted to help Gingrich carry out his new reforms during the ambitious one hundred first days of the new Congress. Ehlers, who was already hailed as the resident nerd, was asked to wire up the House's computers to the Internet, a nerdy assignment to be sure. Ehlers had conducted a similar project for the Michigan legislature, but standardizing all eleven thousand computers on Capitol Hill and eliminating the typewriters in one year would be no small feat.[84] Ehlers told an interviewer, "When I got here, it was easier for me to send an email from my office to Moscow than to send it from my office to an office 20 feet down the hall."[85] Nevertheless, he completed the project on time. The success labeled him as *the* member to approach about science and technology questions; he had made a strategic step in gaining the respect he needed.

"Nonsense Detector"

Ehlers adopted substantial responsibilities throughout his time in Congress. Following the ambitious routine he had established in the Michigan legislature, Ehlers sat on four congressional committees, rather than the average two, for all of his full sessions in Congress. Ehlers's "**nonsense detector**," as he like to call it, and work ethic were an asset for any committee. His involvement peaked during the 109th Congress (2005–2007), which serves as a fine example of the variety of Ehlers's congressional committees.

- During the 109th Congress, Ehlers was given his only congressional chairmanship: **Chairman of House Administration**, a position that oversees the workings of Capitol Hill.

- He served on the Aviation and Water Resource Management Subcommittees under **Transportation and Infrastructures**.

- Always close to his heart, he was on both the Energy and Environment and also the Technology and Standards Subcommittees under the **Science Committee**.

- As a former teacher, he sat on the **Education** subcommittees on Twenty-First-Century Competitiveness and Education Reform.

- Ehlers was chair of the **Joint Committee on the Library** and vice chair of the **Joint Committee on Printing**.

"An Excruciating Moral Decision": Iraq Votes in 2002 and 2007

For Ehlers, the most challenging parts of congressional legislation were not the workload or the long hours (he was used to that) but the decisions that challenged his Micah 6:8 values. Ehlers claimed the most difficult choice he made in congress was the vote on President George W. Bush's decision to invade Iraq. Ehlers, who called himself "slightly pacifist by nature,"[86] feared the loss of life that might come from the decision.

In January 2002, the Bush administration began preparing to widen the scope of US involvement in the Middle East to Iraq. In the following months, the administration justified a preemptive military invasion to Congress based first on the threat of Saddam Hussein's regime and second on the purported presence of weapons of mass destruction in Iraq. Many members quickly supported the war, but Ehlers was not one of them. A *USA Today* article singles out Ehlers and three other congressional members who were particularly uncertain about the vote.[87] An invasion signaled a reversal of US foreign policy: instead of waiting to take the first punch, the US would strike first, a switch that made many representatives uncomfortable. Ehlers questioned the evidence of weapons of mass destruction; true to his academic nature, he didn't want to make an uninformed decision. The war was also unpopular among many of his constituents, who wanted to know why the US was acting now.

Ehlers decided to broach his questions and his constituents' concerns to the president himself. The final draft of a much-edited letter was sent to President Bush on September 27, 2002—just weeks before the vote. After a brief introduction, Ehlers launched into his questions. Near the end of letter, he writes,

> Clearly the attacks of September 2001 demonstrate that the
> Cold War foreign policy doctrines of containment and deter-
> rence are no longer sufficient in our war against terrorism.
> However, I have not seen evidence that demonstrates that
> Saddam is linked to either the events of September 11 or to
> al Qaeda. Recent reports that Iraq has sheltered members of
> al Qaeda in Baghdad and trained others in chemical weapons
> development suggest an alliance, but what is the quality of this

intelligence? What other evidence exists that suggests a long-term partnership? In addition, is there reliable evidence that demonstrates that Saddam intends to provide al Qaeda with weapons of mass destruction for use against the United States or that he intends to use them himself?[88]

Ehlers ends the letter with questions about the future. What diplomatic tactics will the US use in its approach to Iraq? "What plans," he wrote, "are in place for maintaining regional stability during and after military action?"[89]

In answer to these questions, Ehlers had several meetings with members of the Bush administration before the vote. In one particularly persuasive briefing, a physicist from the Pentagon explained Iraq's biological, chemical, and nuclear weapons.[90] Ehlers decided to trust these experts. On October 2, 2002, he voted in favor of the Joint Resolution to Authorize the Use of the United States Armed Forces against Iraq.

The vote upset many of Ehlers's constituents. He attempted to justify his reasons in a statement titled "We Can't Wait for Iraq to Strike First," which was published in the Grand Rapids Press:

> I abhor the idea of the U.S. making a preemptive strike.
> Our philosophy has always been to take the first punch before
> we act. But when the first punch can destroy a city and kill
> hundreds of thousands of people, we must consider ways to
> stop that first punch. . . . In this case, I've concluded not acting
> is more dangerous than acting.[91]

Given the evidence presented to him, Ehlers made a decision that he believed would present the least risk to civilians, the decision most in keeping with Micah 6:8. But the decision unsettled him. He called the vote an "excruciating moral decision."[92] Later, based on more accurate information, Ehlers admitted he regretted his vote. Four years later the *Grand Rapids Press* reported, "He [Ehlers] based his vote on what he now says was faulty evidence of Iraq's ability to produce nuclear weapons, and said the U.S. should have been 'more cautious.'"[93]

Bush's decision to send surge troops to Iraq in 2007 dredged up similar frustrations and concerns for Ehlers and his constituents. Once again, Ehlers found himself faced with a potentially devastating decision, angry constituents, and conflict with his party. In a House hearing about the vote, Ehlers betrayed some of his academic emphasis on appreciating complexity. Congress had been given two options: authorize more troops or maintain the status quo. Ehlers said he wished he could instead vote for a "surge of diplomacy."[94] In a House hearing, he stated,

> I am extremely disappointed that we only have this one
> simplistic, inadequate statement before us for consideration—
> no alternatives, no other ideas, no solutions. The situation
> in Iraq is complicated, and the American people deserve far
> more from Congress than a resolution that essentially calls for
> the status quo.[95]

Regardless, Ehlers did vote in favor of the president's surge troops, despite the war's unpopularity among his constituents and his own dissatisfaction. This time, some of his constituents responded more aggressively.

On a cold March morning, a small group of mostly college students organized a protest in front of the Ehlerses' home on Morningside Drive.[96] From their front window, Jo and Vern could see the group bundled up in coats and brandishing signs with a variety of slogans: "Peace," "Troops Out Now," and "Capitalism Kills." A few activists even taped a sign on the Ehlerses' front door. The Grand Rapids police arrested four of the protesters. While Ehlers had received some criticism and bad press, this was the first public unrest so close to home. Ehlers explained to reporters that he knew the war was unpopular but believed that since Americans were already in Iraq, we had a moral obligation to finish the job and leave the country in better shape with a cohesive plan for the future.

The Financial Crisis

When the financial crisis hit the States in 2008, the whole country suffered, but for many Michiganders, life became desperate. Ehlers succinctly captured the severity of the crisis in Michigan with his go-to line: "When the county catches a cold, Michigan catches pneumonia."[97] Michigan's manufacturers and small business owners within almost every sector of industry felt the pressure of the crisis. Constituents inundated Ehlers's offices with concerns and questions about how they would make ends meet under this new financial stress. "It was tough for Vern to see the economic difficulties his constituents were facing," recalls Jeremy Dalpiaz, a former staffer.[98] But he never avoided his constituents. He intentionally carved out time in his schedule to meet with people struggling with the change in their finances. Ehlers genuinely wanted to understand what his constituents were going through so that he could make the best-informed decisions on their behalf.

Ehlers supported both the General Motors bailout and the use of federal funds to stabilize Wall Street. His justifications stemmed directly from information from constituents. In a guest column in the Grand Rapids Press, he explained,

> I voted for the economic stabilization package because the
> consequences of doing nothing would have been devastating
> for people in our area, I have spoken with many people in
> West Michigan who shared stories with me about hardships
> they are already experiencing due to the credit crisis.[99]

The column includes examples of specific problems mentioned by constituents. Ehlers, a child of the Great Depression, was eager to offer his constituents as much support as he could. He ends the piece by affirming his loyalty to the people he represents.

> I lived through the Great Depression, and it was horrible. I do
> not want anyone in West Michigan, or anywhere else in America,
> to suffer in that way again. I will continue to work diligently in
> Congress to make sure this situation never happens again.[100]

This is not to say Ehlers had no qualms about federal funds being pumped into the economy. He was concerned with the long-term effects of such an expenditure, and one bailout in particular made the usually mild-mannered Ehlers righteously angry.

The American International Group Incorporated (AIG), an insurance service, was bailed out for $180 billion in late 2008. After receiving $85 billion of this money, AIG immediately spent $400,000 on a company retreat to California. Ehlers was incensed. He sent a "Dear Colleagues" letter to the House. It was short, not sweet, and got right to the point. Several members—Republican and Democrat—signed the letter in a rare moment of bipartisan support and shared outrage. Dalpiaz remembers that he rarely saw Ehlers upset about anything, "But this really bothered him."[101] Ehlers saw AIG's spending as an affront to his constituents, American taxpayers who were unjustly suffering for financial mistakes they had not committed.

In looking back on his career, Ehlers was proudest of his accomplishments at the state level, not in Congress. Ehlers often said he didn't consider himself a natural politician. He could correctly identify the flaws of his party, as evidenced in his comment in "Up in Michigan" in 1994, and hold forth a vision for a "surge of diplomacy" in 2007. But he wasn't the person to craft such diplomacy or lead his party toward progress.

Some of his critics have argued that Ehlers could have been in a strategic position to nudge his party toward change. Unlike some of his colleagues, Ehlers didn't need to worry about reelection; his West Michigan seat was one of the safest in the house. With that security, he could have been less of a party man and more of a voice for change. Others have made the claim that Ehlers would have been more effective had he stayed in state politics. The political machinations of Congress presented too steep of a learning curve to someone without his political training.

However, Ehlers could not have had the political success he did without a certain amount of skill. His former staffers were quick to attest that Ehlers had competently and intelligently navigated politics and that he had worked hard to maintain positive relationships with the party leadership so he could get the most done for his constituents. Undoubtedly, Ehlers knew how to take criticism like a politician. His response to the protesters on his doorstep in 2007 is telling. He wasn't angry or even annoyed. He told reporters, "Isn't it great that people feel free to come and demonstrate in front of their congressman's house?"[102] At the end of the day, Ehlers's emphasis on doing justice, loving mercy, and walking humbly kept him focused on the future, the greater good, in spite of the challenges that will inevitably appear on a congressman's doorstep. Willingness to listen was one of the greatest gifts Ehlers gave his constituents—critics and supporters alike acknowledge this much

On behalf of his constituents, Ehlers stuck to his policy strengths, where he knew he could do the most good. He plugged away at meticulous but important legislative work: environmental protection, science policy, and STEM education, all fields that usually only get attention when something goes very wrong. Despite the glacial pace of policy change and often thankless hours of work, Ehlers didn't become cynical. He kept focusing on justice and mercy, and the lengthy, intricate legislation brought out his best characteristics as a politician: efficiency, steadiness, and cool, level-headed compassion.

CHAPTER FOUR
"Leave it better than you found it": Ehlers's Environmental Legacy

When he was a professor at Calvin, Ehlers had personally designed and maintained the photography dark room on campus. With idiosyncratic thoroughness, he created a list of seventy-seven rules governing the use of the dark room, which students routinely ignored. The dark room was always messy. "Finally," Ehlers recalled in a commencement speech, "I tore down all 77 rules and put up just one sheet of paper which said 'Leave it better than you found it.' I told students if they didn't follow that rule they would lose their darkroom privileges. Suddenly the dark room became spotless. It occurred to me that this statement is an excellent rule for all of life."[103] He continued:

> When going for a hike, pick up cans and bottles, so that
> you make sure that the path is better than when you turned
> down it. When you attend a meeting, try to give suggestions
> and address moral issues to assure that the results are more
> Christ-like. When you entertain friends, be sure they are
> enlightened and edified by your conversation.[104]

This sense of responsibility governed Ehlers's life and attitude, and it contextualizes his longest commitment as a public servant: caring for the environment.

Ehlers took geeky pleasure in science-fiction visions of a future world: Would society advance into a sleek and clean utopia or waste away, civilization engulfed by trash? Would we take responsibility now or suffer later? The answer for Ehlers stemmed from his professional concern as a scientist and from his Christian convictions. Ehlers faithfully committed to caring for the environment; he realized one way to serve Christ and his world was by taking care of it. Ehlers developed an interest in "earthkeeping" early in his career and carried those goals into all his levels of office.

Earth Day and *Earthkeeping*

Ehlers became one of West Michigan's earliest adopters and advocates for environmental protection. When the Ehlers family moved to Grand Rapids, Ehlers quickly got involved in the region's environmentalist movement. He helped found the West Michigan Environmental Action Council (WMEAC) in 1968, which still provides environmental programming and advocacy in West Michigan.[105] As the liaison between WMEAC and Calvin College, Ehlers participated in the official beginning of the modern environmental movement in America—the first Earth Day, April 22, 1970.[106] Regular classes at Calvin were canceled on that day so that students could attend special lectures on the environment and attend a rally downtown in the evening. Calvin College students joined thousands of other concerned citizens from colleges, universities, businesses, and special interest groups across the country at rallies and teach-ins focused on the environment. That first Earth Day led to the first wave of environmental legislation in the 1970s.

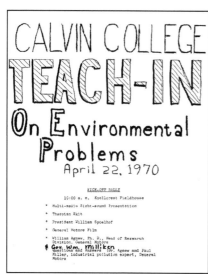

Poster promoting
Calvin College Activities for
Earth Day, April 22, 1970

Ehlers was also instrumental in introducing environmental concerns into his faith community. The energy crisis of the '70s had pushed concerns about the environment to the forefront of many people's minds. Partially in response to this shift in culture, Calvin's new Center for Christian Scholarship (CCCS) dedicated its inaugural project to studies of environmental stewardship. The interdisciplinary project spanned the 1977–78 school year and brought Christian scholars from several different schools and disciplines into a year of thoughtful exploration of this problem. The opportunity put Ehlers on the cutting edge of Christian environmental thought. Besides Ehlers, the team included Calvin professors Peter De Vos (philosophy) and Eugene Dykema (economics), Loren Wilkinson (professor of English, Seattle Pacific College),

Earthkeeping, 1980

Calvin De Witt (professor of environmental studies, University of Wisconsin-Madison), and two student researchers. Their project culminated in the book *Earthkeeping: Christian Stewardship of Natural Resources* (1980).

In charting a new course for Christian engagement with environmental issues, Earthkeeping also served as a response to popular accusations that Christians in the West were largely responsible for the devastating misuse of natural resources. This idea was famously promulgated in a 1967 article by Lynn S. White, titled "The Historical Roots of Our Ecologic Crisis." Francis Schaeffer was the first evangelical voice to take up the debate with elements of White's hypothesis with his book *Pollution and the Death of Man* (1970).[108] *Earthkeeping* continued Shaeffer's progress, suggesting that Christianity has strong implicit imperatives to care for the earth. When the earth suffers, the poor will bear the brunt of the consequences, and Christians should be conservationists because Christ calls his followers to care for the poor and love their neighbors.[109] The project

Excerpts from "A Scientist's Confession of Faith"

Ehlers's Christianity and his love of science went hand in hand. He articulated some of his thoughts on the subject in this "confession."

I believe in God. This is a matter of faith, not a scientific discovery. However, I believe that my scientific knowledge and understanding adds immeasurably to the richness of my faith.

I believe that God has chosen to reveal Himself. He has done so in two specific ways: first of all, through His inspired Scriptures, which we call the Bible, and secondly through the marvelous creation He has made, which provides endless opportunities for scientific study and gives us a valuable philosophical, theological insight.

As a scientist, I often feel that my faith is incredibly strengthened by the scientific discoveries I make and which are made by others. Through science, which is a study of God's creation, we have learned that the world we experience in everyday life with our macroscopic senses is a very small part of the created universe. As we peer into space with telescopes, both optical and radio, we discover the immensity of the universe, and we discern an entirely new world of neutron stars, black holes, and super nebulae, and we come to realize that we are mere specks sitting on a very minor planet circling around a very ordinary star we call the sun, and that there are billions upon billions of stars similar to our sun sprinkled throughout all of space.[107]

brought environmentalism into evangelical circles and effectively introduced the now ubiquitous notion of stewardship into contemporary discussions.[110]

The CCCS project exposed Ehlers to a deeper understanding of environmental questions, but, just as crucially, it allowed Ehlers to experience scholarship that immediately applies to a real-world problem. He personally contributed a chapter on energy to the *Earthkeeping* project, and he delivered a related lecture in 1978 entitled "The Energetic Christian." It opened with these scientific, economic, and moral questions:

> If we are to be true to our Christian confession, we must
> examine the entire energy situation from a Christian perspec-
> tive and ask searching, foundational questions. What is a just
> and proper allocation of energy resources? Are some forms
> of energy more Christian to use than others? What direction
> would a Christian North American energy policy take?[111]

Ehlers made the case that energy conservation is a Christian duty. He used an analogy about income, savings, and inheritance to explain responsible conservation. Our income comes from the sun. We find savings in the plants that have captured the sun's energy, and we inherit a limited amount of natural gases and minerals that we should not squander.[112] If this were money, the fiscally responsible action would be to increase the income and savings and to tap the inheritance only in an emergency. Ehlers said Christians should apply such thinking to energy use.

This pattern of interdisciplinary study and real-world applications gave Ehlers a taste for making tangible changes in the world outside the lab. Before he began the CCCS project, Ehlers was asked whether he thought the work would change his academic interests. He answered no but later admitted that this work had had a profound influence on his life. He wrote in a letter,

> Participation with the multidisciplinary research team, as
> well as the awakening of an environmental conscientiousness
> which had been simmering in the back of my mind for a
> long time, led me not only into concentrating my research
> activities on energy conservation (rather than on nuclear
> and atomic physics) but also stimulated considerably greater
> civic involvement on my part. This eventually led to greater
> participation in my governmental role, and my eventual
> election as a state legislator.
>
> In other words, my CCCS activities not only changed my
> research career, but even led me into politics (a mixed
> blessing at best!).[113]

Ehlers would carry the thoughts and conclusions taken from the *Earthkeeping* project all the way to Capitol Hill. Thirty years later, he was still using his income, savings, and inheritance analogy to discuss energy, no longer with students but with constituents and members of Congress, or at a caucus discussing peak oil.

"If Energy Were Purple"

Ehlers often used quirky analogies to explain complex science legislation. When talking about energy, one of his favorite analogies was asking his audience to imagine if energy were purple.

Most people in the world, particularly from America, do not understand energy the way they should. It's very difficult. You can't touch it, you can't see it, you can't smell it, etc. You can see the effects of it, but you can't see the energy itself. That's part of the problem when you are dealing with energy. . . .

I wish energy were purple. If energy were purple, you could see it. If you drove up to your house in the winter, you would see a sort of blue haze coming through the walls and little purple rivulets coming out around the windows and the doors. You would say, "Good grief! I have to insulate this house better. I have to seal the doors and windows." If you do it, you'll save a lot of money, but you'll also save a lot of energy. I know because I've done it—and our utility bills dropped by 33%— that's worth doing.

Similarly, if you drove down the highway, you might see a little hybrid car with just a tiny little bit of purple coming out of it. And behind that a giant SUV with such a big cloud of purple around it, you can't even tell what make it is You might say, "Hey! I need to go down to the dealer and take a look at those hybrids."

So part of the problem with energy is that we don't understand it. Another problem is some people don't *want* to understand it. That is one of biggest problems I fight in the Congress—the preconceived notion that oil or fossil fuels are the answer and that if we can just get more of them, we can solve the problem.[114]

A Conservative in Every Conservationist

Even as a young scientist, Ehlers naturally gravitated toward discussions about science in the public arena. He read widely, gathering clippings and articles about his favorite science and political topics. He became active in professional networks that gave him opportunities to serve on nationally recognized committees. For instance, in 1973, he was on the American Physical Society's first selection committee for its congressional fellowship, and throughout the late '70s he was a member of the Panel on Public Affairs.[115] He also was appointed to a panel assigned to evaluate the National Bureau of Standards (now the National Institute of Standards and Technology).

The theme of environmentalism ran through all of Ehlers's political career, beginning with his days as a science advisor to Congressman Gerald Ford. Besides that, Ehlers was a member in 1970 on Governor Milliken's task force dedicated to the environment. Later, in 1982, Ehlers worked specifically on the governor's Toxic Substance Control Commission.[116] In the state legislature, Ehlers was instrumental in passing wetland protection acts that were stricter than the current federal laws.[117] In Congress, Ehlers submitted bill after bill that addressed pollution, proposed more oversight and a bigger budget for the EPA, and combated invasive species in the Great Lakes.

This dedication to the environment set Ehlers apart within his own party.[118] Ehlers tried to counter the perception of the Republican party as "un-green" with the quip, "There's a conservative in every conservationist."[119] However, his environmental conscience often led him to break with the party line. In 1995, he went head to head with both fellow House Republicans and the Republican governor of Michigan, John Engler. The bill in question made compliance to EPA regulations for the Great Lakes states voluntary, rather than mandatory.[120] Ehlers drafted revisions in the language of the bill. He was concerned that the word voluntary left too big a loophole; some states could potentially wriggle out of their commitment to keeping the Great Lakes clean. Ehlers's amendment passed by a tiny margin—twenty-seven to twenty-four—but it was hailed as a notable success for the future of the Great Lakes. Only a few days later, Engler and other Great Lakes governors suggested their own language for the bill, circumventing the wishes of legislators who agreed with Ehlers. Engler and the other governors favored the voluntary language, and the final vote confirmed the governors' changes and not Ehlers's amendments.

Ehlers's record is full of such examples. A few months later, Ehlers once again cast a vote for the "wrong" side of the aisle. This time he was among forty-nine Republicans who had voted to eliminate seventeen "overly restrictive provisions from the appropriations bill for the Environmental Protection Agency."[121] "The bill as written really almost guts the ability of the EPA to do anything," Ehlers told a reporter.[122] After another close vote, this amendment also failed in the House. In 2001, Ehlers broke with all of the Michigan Republican delegation and voted against President Bush's energy plan; he objected because the plan loosened oil exploration regulations and allowed drilling in the Arctic. This time he was one among only thirty-five Republicans.[123]

Supporting the environment could also put Ehlers at loggerheads with some of his constituents. While Michigan tends to be an environmentally friendly state, the state's even friendlier stance on business can sometimes present a conflicting priority. Ehlers was awarded the Michigan Environmental Council's Helen and William Milliken's Distinguished Service Award in 2006, in large part for his support of "higher fuel economy standards in cars."[124] He was the only member of the Michigan delegation to support the standards, and the Big Three were not pleased. As Ehlers told the *Grand Rapids Press,* "They accused me of killing the auto industry."[125] But the decision won him points with Michigan's environmentalists.

Ehlers plants a tree during a Habitat for Humanity event held in the 500 block of Jefferson Street in Grand Rapids, June 6, 1998

The Third Coast: Fighting for the Great Lakes

Ehlers's greatest accomplishment in environmental policy,[126] and perhaps one of his most tangible legacies in West Michigan, were the Great Lakes Legacy Act of 2002 and the Great Lakes Legacy Reauthorization Act of 2008.[127] Ehlers sponsored both acts. He had joined the Great Lakes Task Force in Congress during the '90s. It took many years to thoroughly study the problem, prepare solutions, and craft the legislation before the task force members saw the fruits of their labor. This legislation required all of Ehlers's skills of strategy and his strength as someone who could work behind the scenes to get several different parties to work together. Any Great Lakes legislation affects many different players: the various state governments, the Canadian government, local business, county and local officials, and private citizens. Kerry Duggan, deputy director and development director at the Michigan League of Conservation Voters, praised Ehlers for this often-overlooked gift—Ehlers the scientist, conservationist, and politician was not afraid to spend time on complex issues, and the Great Lakes initiatives were anything but simple.[128]

The EPA has dubbed the Great Lake Legacy Acts a "tremendous success."[129] When they were finally authorized, the Legacy Acts of 2002 authorized $270 million for the cleanup of toxic hot spots that the EPA had identified. The Great Lakes Legacy Reauthorization Act of 2008 ensured that the work has continued. Subsequently, the EPA has invested $338 million into cleaning the Great Lakes and continues to study and decontaminate trouble spots, greatly improving the health of the ecological regions. The Legacy Acts were particularly successful because they encouraged strong partnership across all levels of governments—state, federal, local—and within the corporate world.[130] Ehlers knew that only a unified effort on all fronts could bring about environmental change.

Ehlers's environmental record, while very good, was not perfect, according to some green agency watchdogs. He received endorsement from the Sierra Club during most of his time in Congress, but not every term. While he was outspoken about alternative fuels, he supported nuclear power, which was viewed in some quarters as too environmentally risky.[131] Ehlers kept his comments on climate change quiet through most of his career, to the annoyance of his more liberal constituents. He never denied the existence of climate change, but it was only at the end of his career that he talked about the human causation of climate change. He would discuss the subject if asked about it pointedly, especially if his colleagues had questions. In a radio interview, Ehlers recounted a story of an interaction he had had with a fellow congressman he sat next to at a breakfast. This particular member of Congress did not believe in climate change. He turned to Ehlers and asked, "Hey Vern, is there carbon dioxide in this room?" Vern replied yes and proceeded to explain where it came from. " I think in that twenty-minute conversation, I made him doubt his opinion that global warming was just a farce," said Ehlers, "He realized there was scientific basis."[132]

On his retirement, members of the environmental activism community claimed Ehlers had had a significant hand in making the Great Lakes America's "third coast." Michigan state senator Patty Birkholz, chairwoman of the nonpartisan Great Lakes Legislative Caucus, praised Ehlers's contributions, telling the *Great Lakes Echo,*

> He has been so effective and persistent in dealing with Great
> Lakes issues, certainly from a scientific point of view, from an
> ecological sustainability point of view and regarding the health
> of the entire Great Lakes. . . . He's been just fantastic as a fed-
> eral legislator and we're going to miss him a whole lot.[133]

Ehlers's commitment to the environment ran deep. One of his staffers said, "It was important for him to make sure I understood that we have a responsibility to take care of the environment, not as a Republican, but as a Christian."[134] Christian duty came first, and party loyalty came later. In keeping with his Christian Reformed thinking, Ehlers believed caring for the present world has spiritual ramifications in the kingdom yet to come. These profound beliefs motivated Ehlers to chip away at the persistent problems of environmental policy.

CHAPTER FIVE
A Scientist in the House:
Ehlers and Science Policy

In a 1969 letter to a publisher of science textbooks, Ehlers outlined attributes that every good science textbook needs; at the top of the list was "relevance."

> Any general textbook . . . must be relevant to all other disciplines, and to life itself. This does not mean that one should, as an example, spend an entire physical science course discussing the moral implications of nuclear weaponry; rather, it simply means that one should be cognizant of the interest in these moral questions and should use this interest as a springboard for discussion. . . . My point is simply that physics *is* relevant to today's world, and both our instructors and textbooks should be aware of this and capitalize on it.[135]

Ehlers also argued that science textbooks need to be based on thoroughly researched, sound science. That science should also be integrated, connected to real-world application and ramifications. In the letter, Ehlers argues that good science texts need to be "self-aware of the nature of science," "sensitive to the philosophical, theological and moral issues connected to science," and "humorous (because 'Science *is* enjoyable')." Ehlers understood that if we want science to improve people's lives, we must be prepared for the complicated moral, ethical, and social issues that arise with every scientific innovation.

Even though the majority of Ehlers's career was not spent actually doing physics, science was his chief and abiding passion and always relevant to his sense of vocation. Ehlers was fascinated by how science works in the world, and he wanted to be in on the action.

However, getting his congressional colleagues excited about science was uphill work. Ehlers became painfully aware of the scientific ignorance among the very people making big decisions about science policy. There were not enough qualified scientists speaking into the legislative process and not enough science-savvy citizens who would hold their leaders to higher standards. With an increasingly science-dependent economy, the gaps between scientists, policy makers, and citizens would only become more difficult and more important to bridge.

As a scientist, legislator, and educator, Ehlers felt uniquely equipped to act as that bridge. In 1997, Ehlers was asked to work on a new United States science policy. A quick survey of the policy reveals Ehlers's understanding of the place of science in policy and the specific elements of scientific history he considered the most important. Ehlers frequently returned to many of the same themes he had highlighted in years past during his years as professor: science needs to be relevant, integrated, self-aware, and continually evolving through education.

Unlocking Our Future: Ehlers's Science Policy Proposal

Thirty years after his letter about what makes a good science textbook, Ehlers was asked to write a different sort of textbook—not for children, but for an infinitely more wily, varied, and reticent audience: the United States House of Representatives. Ehlers suggested to Newt Gingrich that the government's current science policy needed work. In the '90s, most scientific decisions still operated under the guidelines laid out by Vannevar Bush, an inventor and science administrator, in the fifty-year-old policy manual *Science, the Endless Frontier*. Ehlers felt this old policy had not kept up with the times. Americans had made enormous innovations in the past fifty years, but, as Ehlers wrote in his policy, "no entity as vast, interconnected, and diverse as the science and engineering enterprise can successfully operate on autopilot perpetually."[136] Ehlers's new science policy, *Unlocking Our Future: Toward a New Science Policy*, or, as it was often called,

Unlocking our Future: Toward a New National Science Policy, 1998

"The Ehlers Report," marks Ehlers's attempt to place himself in the larger history of science policy in America. The project tested his ability not only to understand the nature and current role of science but also to envision how science should adapt to a changing world.

A new science policy was a good fit in Gingrich's plan to reform the House in the 1990s. Gingrich presented Ehlers with a threefold task: rewrite the United States science policy, address science and math education, and serve as a liaison between the scientific community and Congress.[137] The science policy project was formally introduced at a science roundtable on October 27, 1997. In his opening remarks, Gingrich emphasized the need to reenvision science in the new millennium. Government officials needed a better understanding of science so they could invest in the best scientific enterprises. The Gingrich charter declared, "You give me a mission large enough to mobilize the nation. You give me a set of strategic investments large enough to be worth doing, and then make it my problem to go out and figure out how to find the money."[138] Vannevar Bush's original policy had guaranteed that the government would always fund research; the question for the twenty-first century was, *how* can legislators determine which projects are worthy of investment?

Historical Context: Three Stages of Science in the US

Ehlers's report does not deviate drastically from Vannevar Bush's policy. In fact, Ehlers called the project a "fine-tuning" rather than a rewriting,[139] and he saw his overall proposal as a natural heir to Bush's. Ehlers divided the history of science research into three "mega eras."[140] During the first era, roughly from Ben Franklin to Ernest Lawrence (d. 1958), the government benignly ignored scientific research.[141] Private donors funded their own projects, which were often for agricultural ends. Bush wrote a policy for a post–World War and Cold War America, ushering in the second "mega era" of science. During the war, scientists, working quietly in universities across the country, realized nuclear technology could end the war. The difficulty was bridging the big gap between the scientific community and Washington. The government had little to do with science, and scientists had no good way of channeling their ideas and contributions into the public or military sectors. The mid-war scramble for an atomic bomb made it plain that the US needed an organized interface between its government and its scientists.

By the end of WWII, electrical engineer Vannevar Bush had become a key power broker in all matters relating to wartime science. As a close advisor to President Roosevelt through the time of the Manhattan Project, he had seen first-hand how science, technology, research, and defense had become inextricably linked.[142] He naturally became the chief advocate for the development of a federal science policy. In 1944, Roosevelt commissioned Bush to write an official document that would outline a policy allowing the government to sponsor and promote scientific innovation. Roosevelt asked Bush to explore four questions: What knowledge, gained in confidential military efforts during the war, can be released to the public for the general welfare? How can we continue to fight the "war on disease"? How can the government aid research? And, finally, what is the best method for developing the talent of young American scientists in order to keep America competitive? Bush's policy was distinctly militaristic. When discussing FDR's first question about how science promotes the general welfare, Bush jumped immediately to a national security justification for science. Then the science policy turned inward to address the well-being of the nation. Bush spoke of science as "an unexplored hinterland,"[143] suggesting that the nation must harness untapped scientific resources in order to ensure its own security, health, and flourishing.

Bush's overall conclusion, in answer to President Roosevelt's questions, was that the United States needed a "mechanism," or some organization, accessible to both scientists and government liaisons, that would be primarily a medium for supporting basic research. After several years of legislative negotiations, Bush's proposal led to the National Science Foundation Act of 1950, which established the NSF as an institution and set the stage for US science to flourish during the second half of the twentieth century.

The NSF became a prominent fixture during the Cold War years, but—as Ehlers tells it—neither the public nor Congress fully appreciated the need for basic research. The late twentieth century witnessed an incredible acceleration in technological advancement, which further muddied the relationship between basic science, applied science, and the economy. Ehlers was quick to point out the differences between Bush's time and his own: "We no longer are fighting the Cold War. . . . Our competition with other nations is, by and large, no longer military; it is economic."[144]

Ehlers claimed that by the dawn of the new millennium, America was in a third "mega era" in science policy. His report was intended as an outline of what the US would need to do in this third era. He reasserted many of Bush's claims, especially the necessity of basic research, but he acknowledged that the landscape of research had grown more complex.

Science in the Third Era: Three Suggestions from *Unlocking Our Future*

In *Unlocking Our Future*, Ehlers offers three overarching suggestions for improving science in the new millennium: he reemphasizes the necessity of basic research; explains the importance of developing places for the government, science, and the private sector to benefit from innovation; and encourages a strengthened science/math education curriculum. Ehlers's suggestions echo the thoughts he had about the importance and nature of science back in the late '60s. The reemphasis of basic research is a call to pursue sound science. The complicated nature of science comes to bear when we consider how scientific innovation interacts with the economy; for Ehlers, science is an integrated enterprise that affects other spheres of life. Ehlers felt the need to remind Congress of what science can and cannot do—scientific endeavors must be self-aware. Finally, Ehlers demonstrates his belief in the fundamental necessity of science education. Science begins in a classroom, and so, in order for the US to remain innovative, science education must flourish first.

"The Two Cultures"

Throughout his career, Ehlers lamented what he considered the rampant scientific ignorance of average American citizens and even members of Congress. All three of Ehlers's suggestions in *Unlocking Our Future* boil down to a fundamental problem he called "the Two Cultures." Scientist and author C. P. Snow coined the phrase in the 1950s to describe the disconnect between the science community and other disciplines. Snow writes,

> *Constantly, I felt that I was moving among two groups of comparable intelligence, identical in race, not grossly different in social origin, earning about the same incomes, who have almost ceased to communicate at all.*[145]

Snow concludes that it is almost as if the two groups spoke a different language and represented different cultures. Ehlers often quoted C. P. Snow specifically when explaining the need for a new science policy. He believed the gap between the groups was getting worse.[146] Ehlers cited polls showing that many American college students didn't know what causes the seasons to change or what direction the stars moved across the sky. What was even more disconcerting was that Ehlers detected the "Two Cultures" problem in the House—among people who were making decisions about science.

Ehlers accepts a certificate naming him a fellow of the American Physical Society from the APS President, Dr. Kumar Patel, October 18, 1995

1 *Basic Research*

As Ehlers was preparing *Unlocking Our Future,* he found that many of his colleagues didn't understand the concepts of basic and applied research. According to Ehlers,

> Congress tends to view them as separate, with basic research as a good but fuzzy thing, and applied research, in general, as not a good thing, and something for the private sector to take care of. Vannevar Bush regarded them as related, and saw the linear relationship between them.[147]

So, in *Unlocking Our Future,* Ehlers tried to set the record straight.

Ehlers affirmed Bush's claim that the best way the government can ensure American scientific innovation is through federal funding for basic research. Bush wrote in *Science, the Endless Frontier*, "Science progress on a broad front results from the free play of intellects, working on subjects of their own choice, in the manner dictated by their curiosity for exploration of the unknown."[148] In other words, basic research explores for discovery, not for a preconceived result. Conversely, applied research is motivated by a product goal. Naturally, the private sector will often fund applied research, but basic research is a tougher sell. The government needs to ensure that the basic research will get funding.

Ehlers explained to his colleagues that basic science and applied science are dependent on each other. He used the terms *understanding-driven research* and *use-inspired research.* Sometimes research for the sake of understanding can aid in the development of new technology, and sometimes a new technological innovation can aid to our understanding of a scientific phenomenon. Together, the findings of basic and applied science projects can produce knowledge and results.[149]

2   *Connections between Science, Government, and the Market*

Once Ehlers had established the necessity of basic research, the next question was one particularly important to the twenty-first century: How can the government facilitate interactions between basic research and the market (and vice versa)? To illustrate this difficulty, Ehlers often spoke of the "Valley of Death" that occurs in the process between a discovery from basic research and the application of that research in a product market. The gap between federal and private funding in research is too wide for the federal government to bridge alone. *Unlocking Our Future* suggests that the private market must proactively regulate research and not leave all the oversight to the government.[150] On the other side, the federal government needs to develop a set of criteria that will help it make scientifically sound judgments about where to send funds. Legislators should make use of peer reviewers, scholars, and experts. This will lend credibility to Congress's ability to make scientific decisions. These operational concerns occupy the entire middle portion of *Unlocking Our Future*.

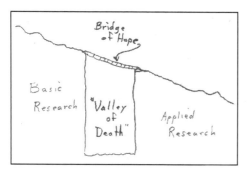

Ehlers's drawing illustrating the "Valley of Death"

However, Ehlers was quick to nuance his claims about the power of science to legitimize legislation. Harkening back to the thoughts he had expressed about the nature of science in the 1960s, Ehlers includes a stern caveat in his science policy about the limitations of science. In a 1969 letter to the publisher of a science textbook, Ehlers wrote,

> Students should be aware of the limitations of science and its methodology. Science is a religion to many people, and perhaps that is why they are afraid to examine these fundamental assumptions and bases; however I believe such analysis is essential in science, just as in any other discipline.[151]

In his document, Ehlers repeated the sentiment, saying, "Science can inform issues, but it cannot decide them."[152] *Unlocking Our Future* cites questions about the environment as a case in point.[153] Science informs us about how pollutants may harm or not harm a certain piece of land, but science cannot tell us how to equitably conserve the land and the rights of a landowner. Also, questions about the environment are complex—they touch on theology, philosophy, morality, economics, and questions of the greater good. In his 1969 letter to the textbook publisher, Ehlers said that most scientists tend to "sweep these questions under the rug." But a scientist who is also a policy maker has no such luxury; science brings with it uncertainty, especially when it comes to legislation that includes several complex systems.

Integrating Science, Life, Justice, and Policy: Cloning

One of the trickiest issues Ehlers faced as a congressman was cloning. Ehlers was in his second full term as a representative when scientists announced that they had successfully cloned a sheep named Dolly. Scientists had been tinkering with genetic experiments for decades, but Dolly brought the moral and social implications of cloning to the public's attention.

For Ehlers, cloning touched on a lot of beliefs he held most dear: his sense of justice, the sanctity of human life, and the power and limitations of science. Ehlers believed most genetic experimentation was very beneficial, and he was a reliable champion of scientific freedom. "However," he wrote, "while the possibilities of scientific experimentation normally are beneficial, there are times when society—through the governmental process—can and should place limits on scientific experimentation."[154] Ehlers was decidedly against the cloning of humans because it does not promote a flourishing life for the potential humans involved. Ehlers insisted on a measured, thoughtful, conscientious examination of what this new science can do and should not do. He ends the article about banning cloning with a statement in keeping with his nuanced view of science and his desire to work toward a just society: ▶

> *We should not go blindly down the twisting path of scientific progress but instead proceed cautiously while carefully scrutinizing the far-reaching implications of human cloning. In light of modern-day society's often flippant attitude about the significance of a human life, we must do all that is possible to tenaciously uphold the dignity of humanity[155]*

Ehlers introduced the first of many batches of anti-cloning legislation; none have been successful, although other countries have banned human cloning. Ehlers's efforts illustrate his commitment to sound and thoughtful science.

 3   STEM Education

The final section of *Unlocking Our Future* addresses the need to bolster math and science education in America. Ehlers argued that the future of any scientific progress relies on a robust science education at every level. This section opens with a quote attributed to Francis Bacon: *nam et ipsa scientia potestas est* (knowledge is power). Bacon was an important figure in Ehlers's conception of science. Earlier in his work at Calvin College, Ehlers had credit Bacon for laying the foundation for "modern" science and articulating the desire for science to harness the power latent within God's creation.[156] Ehlers brought the same logic to *Unlocking Our Future* by emphasizing the necessity of education in any plan that would keep America competitive in an increasingly global economy.

Results of the Science Policy

Ehlers personally spoke to approximately ten thousand scientists and two thousand nonscientists over the course of a year as he crafted *Unlocking Our Future*, and the small staff he employed for this project received over three hundred letters and emails from interested citizens.[157] Astonishingly, Ehlers and his staff completed the policy on time in 1998 and on budget. Everyone commended Ehlers for his work, acknowledging that it was no small undertaking. However, *Unlocking Our Future* achieved mixed and generally tepid results. Many members of the science community were appreciative of Congress's effort to keep reassessing the relationship between science and government, especially Ehlers's reassertion of the importance of basic research and his attention to education.[158] Ehlers's fellow Republicans appreciated the way he articulated the distinction between basic and applied research, because it gave them the language they needed to defend science spending while claiming to be fiscally conservative.[159]

The commissioners of the report, Newt Gingrich and James Sensenbrenner, chair of the House Science Committee, were "cautious" in their praise.[160] At the launch of the document, Gingrich remarked, "This is a very good start, but it really only scratches the surface of what, over the next four or five years, will have to be a very important national dialogue."[161] Gingrich had given Ehlers a visionary task: create "a mission large enough to mobilize the nation" and "a set of strategic investments large enough to be worth doing."[162] Critics believed *Unlocking Our Future* did not actually provide a "strategic set of investments." Sensenbrenner and Ehlers conceded this. Sensenbrenner called it "not a visionary document, but . . . a document for visionaries. After all, that is what scientists are."[163] George Brown (D-CA), the minority leader on the science committee, conscientiously did not endorse the report, because it failed to address issues that he considered important in the future of science research.[164] Brown eschewed Bush's linear model of basic to applied research, arguing that the nation needed a more sophisticated model. He also feared that *Unlocking Our Future* favored the hard sciences to the neglect of the social sciences. Generally, Brown thought the report did not go far enough or offer enough specific tools to help craft a science policy for the future; it essentially supported the status quo. Still other critics wished the report included more constructive pieces of advice about how to promote women and minorities in the sciences and distinct methods for bolstering STEM education.[165]

Ehlers responded by highlighting that the document was designed to give only broad strokes and didn't attempt to offer particularly detailed suggestions. He called the report a "commencement" that he hoped would engender more discussion about the role of science in government. On the floor, Ehlers explained,

The only comments that we received reflecting reservations agree with and support most of the report, but are concerned about what is not in the report. In other words, they believe that we should have gone further, and indeed we should have and would have in certain subject areas had we had the time.[166]

Unlocking Our Future certainly may have encouraged some immediate conversation after its release. But the report seems to have had a short reach. By most accounts, it was principled and well researched, but it lacked an over-arching visionary message, a call to action. It mainly served the majority and the status quo but didn't outline a clear path for future progress. Gingrich, while grateful, wanted more work to be done on science policy. However, he left the House soon after the release of the document, and, without his political presence, the project dwindled.[167]

CHAPTER SIX
Looking for Sputnik: Ehlers and Education

Like many in his generation, Ehlers was inspired by the launch of the first artificial Earth satellite, Sputnik, in 1957.[168] It was the beginning of the space race. This first victory went to the Russians, but, in 1969, the Americans were the first to put a man on the moon. Nationally, the interest in space invigorated science, technology, engineering, and math (STEM) education. However, as Cold War anxieties eventually waned, so did the national emphasis on STEM education. Later in his career, Ehlers decried the national ambivalence by asking the question, "Where is Sputnik when we need it?"[169] Ehlers looked back to the excitement over Sputnik as something we needed to recapture in the American education system. With that golden age in mind, he would work for higher standards in STEM education throughout his entire career. In Congress, this dedication manifested itself in several ways. First, Ehlers never lost his professorial demeanor. He was a kind boss and mentor, and he was eager to educate his constituents about how government works. Second, he willingly took on the role of Congress's go-to, behind-the-scenes science advisor, assisting his colleagues with technical questions and combating the scientific ignorance in the house. Finally, Ehlers put in countless hours crafting STEM legislation, much of which would be included in the America COMPETES Act of 2007.

Ehlers with a different NASA crew, Shuttle mission crew STS-108, 2001

Ehlers and the Hubble Crew

One of Ehlers's staffers, Beth Bandstra-Dekker, reflects on Ehlers's meeting with the Hubble space crew.

One of my proudest moments working for him was when the Hubble space crew came in to testify before the Science and Technology Committee. They presented their research and asked if anyone had questions. But no member had any questions for this group, because no one understood their work, except Vern. He was asking all the questions. The crew was enamored of Vern because he understood what they were doing up there.

Finally, the chairman said, "Well, one committee member had an interest, so why don't we adjourn and he can continue to talk with them," which he did for almost a half an hour.

I remember thinking, this is why we need scientists in Congress. This is why we need people like Vern, a teacher and scientist. It was quite moving to see these incredible people, who had worked on Hubble, and to look at my boss and be amazed at how good he was.

Once a Professor, Always a Professor

As a speaker, Ehlers was not known for his charisma, but he was extremely adept at explaining issues to constituents. As Bandstra-Dekker recalled, "His ability to explain things was remarkable to me."[170] When Bandstra-Dekker later pursued elected office herself, she often turned to Ehlers with questions because of his ability to break down the issues.

Ehlers's leadership within his staff reflected his professorial experience; he was honest with them and clear about what he expected of the team. Many congressional offices had reputations for being high in stress, low in pay, and full of toxic work relationships. But Ehlers operated his office differently. Rather than hiring a large staff and paying them miserably, Ehlers and his chief of staff, Bill McBride, carefully selected a small staff of highly qualified people. Almost everyone in his office had advanced degrees or was at least working on one. McBride recalled, "Other people on the Hill knew his office was a good place to work. And people stayed in their positions with him for years, while a lot of these offices only have people for months or a year."[171]

One Washington staffer, Jeremy Dalpiaz, described his first interview with Ehlers as "unusual." Rather than leading with a question about previous experience, Ehlers's first question was, what book have you finished recently? Ehlers didn't want just anybody working for him; he valued thoughtfulness and people who knew how to deal with complex ideas. Later, Ehlers and McBride accommodated Dalpiaz's schedule so he could finish his master's degree in public policy. On the day he finished his degree, Dalpiaz walked into Ehlers's office to tell him. Without missing a beat, Ehlers exclaimed, "That's wonderful! When will you start your PhD?"[172] Dalpiaz laughed, because the last thing he wanted to do was turn around and start more school work, but he appreciated Ehlers's encouragement. When staffer Rachel ten Haaf was leaving Ehlers's staff to attend graduate school, she remembered Ehlers telling her that it would be competitive but she should not lose sight of what really mattered to her. "He told me to not cede what was right in the face of what was expedient, but just keep working for what I believed was the most important," said ten Haaf, "I follow that dictum to this day."[173] With a teacherly sensitivity, Ehlers encouraged his staff to pursue their full potential.

Ehlers with staff ca. 2005, Left to Right: Bill McBride, Leslee Rohs, Kelli Scholten, Julia Jester, Kevan Chapman, Rachel Fenton, Matt Reiffer, Vern, Ben Gielow, Jenny Ungrey, Matt Evans, Rick Treur, Jennifer Duthler, Jeremy Dalpiaz.

The staff always had access to Ehlers, who kept their avenues of communication with him wide open. He treated his staff with the utmost respect, "And in turn," said Dalpiaz, "we gave him the utmost respect. He was a kind man to work for." He welcomed frank discussions and never dismissed or punished staffers who disagreed with him. Ehlers fostered team unity on annual retreats with both the district and DC staff. On these occasions, the whole staff would meet together in either location to discuss the agenda for the next year. It was a time to air ideas and concerns and get everyone on board for the next year. But when it came time for actual decision making, Ehlers always made up his own mind. He took the notes, research, and arguments of staff seriously, but in the end he drew his own conclusions and made his own judgments. Sometimes the staff didn't even know how he was going to vote when he left the office for the floor, but they trusted him, knowing the justifications for his vote would be based on sound logic.

Besides an interest in supporting their careers, Ehlers took a personal interest in his staff. Dalpiaz said,

He was interested in your family. He wanted to spend time
with us having lunch in the office. He enjoyed going down to
the floor with us and asking us questions. He took time to get
to know who we were. And that is not entirely common.

In retrospective interviews, Ehlers's staffers expressed their gratitude to
their former boss for a positive experience in an environment that was known to
be stressful. Jonathan Hirte claimed, "One of the reasons I stayed on the Hill was
because my experience with Vern and his staff was so wonderful. And I know that
this not always the norm."[174] The goodwill among his staff has had trickle effects
in their ensuing careers. Julia Jester explained, "We all owe him a lot. He and Bill
[McBride] helped us, and we still help each other with things our career, because
we got to know each other so well back then."[175]

Ehlers's role as teacher blossomed in politics. As a state senator and a United
States congressman, he revised or wrote mini-textbooks about how government
works for constituents, high schoolers, and elementary students.[176]

His educational work never
stopped. He believed that the more
people understood about government,
the more likely they would be to get
involved and become good leaders.
He would end many of his speeches to
constituents with the injunction, "Get
involved!" Recalling that his own political involvements were first spurred
by such encouragement, he was quick
to share the same message with the
next generation.

Ehlers would often wear a Cat in the
Hat hat when he visited schools to
read to children.

Alonzo Woodruff Post Office Building

As a congressman, Ehlers loved his interactions with children. He knew that such positive meetings can be informative for a child's understanding about how government works. One particularly "fun" piece of legislation for Ehlers and his staff was the renaming of the Ionia post office, a law that began in a middle school classroom.

In 2007, an eighth-grade social studies class in Ionia, Michigan, unearthed a fascinating bit of local history. Alonzo Woodruff, a Michigan native, had joined the Union army at age 22. He served with distinction and was awarded the Congressional Medal of Honor.[177]

Woodruff settled in Ionia, where his great-great-granddaughters still lived. The class of eighth graders wanted to commemorate Woodruff somehow. So they contacted their congressman, Vern Ehlers, and asked him whether the Ionia post office could be renamed in Woodruff's honor. Ehlers said he would try. A year later on April 23, 2008, H.R. 5479 was passed into law, and the Alonzo Woodruff Post Office Building was born.

As a general rule, Ehlers spent most of his efforts on more difficult and important legislation, but Ehlers saw this as an opportunity to give these students a meaningful experience with their representative, one that he hoped would inform their attitude toward government as adults. Always excited to be a part of the educational process, Ehlers made sure his staff kept the students up-to-date on how their bill was progressing. In their thank-you letters to Ehlers, the Ionia eighth graders explained how much they had learned about how bills become laws through this experience.

Science behind the Scenes

Sponsoring earth-shattering or visionary legislation was never Ehlers's goal as he entered politics. He had formidable skills when it came to getting things done as well as a knack for positioning himself in the right place at the right time. But when it comes to his legacy in government, Ehlers's accomplishments were quiet initiatives that often had nothing to do with legislation. Much of Ehlers's value as legislator was his ability to educate.

Reflecting his own vocational switch from science to politics, Ehlers thought of his fellow scientists as prime recruits for public service. There simply weren't enough scientists in government to juggle all of the science-related questions and legislation that flowed through the House every day. Fellow legislators desperately needed Ehlers's advice, even though he was not a party leader or the chair of the Science and Technology Committee. Doug Koopman, a professor of political science at Calvin and some-time congressional aide, recalled how Ehlers came to fill a behind-the-scenes scientific advisory role. Koopman said, "Nobody understood science like Congressman Ehlers," and, because he was a straight-talking, honest, no-nonsense sort of operator, he was good person to ask.[178]

Ehlers's mere presence could sometimes make a big difference. Once, he was watching the floor debate from his office, when a member began talking about cutting funding for ATMs. The congressman who was speaking was thinking about bank machines, but Ehlers realized the bill in discussion concerned Asynchronous Transfer Mode—a computer function. Ehlers literally ran to the floor to keep the whole House from becoming a laughing stock.[179] Many legislative decisions are influenced by aides, who may not actually know anything about science, or by lobbyists, who will offer good but biased information. Sometimes the information is just faulty, which made Ehlers's "nonsense detector" an important asset on the Hill.

Ehlers gladly accepted this teacherly role in Congress, but it was a difficult and often solitary job. Scientists and policy makers frequently miscommunicate and misunderstand each other. Ehlers was a reliable bridge between the two. He spoke to the scientific community, encouraging his scientist colleagues to join him in Congress. This was his personal solution to the "Two Cultures" problem—teach each side about the other. Ehlers told an audience of AAAS members,

Everyone respects me as a scientist. . . . They listen carefully to what I have to say—but when it comes to *believing* it, it's a different matter. . . . I've learned over the years that if another member of Congress comes to me and asks me a question about science and I give them an answer which as far as I know is scientifically correct, and if the answer I give that person agrees with the previous assumptions the person has made about it, I am the world's greatest scientist, and they will go around quoting me to other members. . . . However, if my statement disagrees with their intrinsic, intuitive belief, I'm a lousy scientist and they will never quote me[180]

Then, Ehlers appealed to his audience of scientists, "It's really an unfair battleground, and I hope you'll join me wherever possible in correcting that in conversations. It is not easy, it's not always polite, but usually . . . with a little jocularity, you can make your point without angering people too much."[181] Ehlers feared his work on bridging the gap would come to an end unless more scientists rolled up the sleeves of their lab coats and got involved in politics.

STEM Education

Ehlers worked to bridge the gap between science and policy makers through legislation near and dear to his heart, especially in the area of math and science education. Like his interest in the environment, Ehlers's commitment to education was long-standing. He had a particular interest in preparing teachers to serve at the K–12 levels. One of his enduring contributions to Calvin College's curriculum was his development of science education courses. Despite a large physics course load, Ehlers invested significant time and energy into learning about elementary and secondary science education. He took time to learn education jargon and worked closely with the education department to craft a course that would give teachers the right sort of tools to give their students quality science education, even in elementary school.[182] Looking back, he was proud of the education course and believed it had made a difference.

Ehlers carried the fight for education to Congress. In his speeches and interviews with teachers and policy makers, Ehlers shared statistics which showed that American science education was "wide but not deep." In 2000, "only 69% of high school science and mathematics teachers had a degree in the subject they teach, and 18% of current science teachers neither majored nor minored in science."[184] A 1998 international study revealed that high school seniors in United States were dead last in physics.[185] These statistics concerned Ehlers because he feared that the American education system would not produce enough good scientists to keep America competitive, an issue he addressed in his science policy report.

Dr. Ehlers teaching a demonstration class, late '60s / early '70s

He was likewise concerned for the students who would not become scientists but still needed a general working knowledge of math and science. Echoing the same sentiments that C. P. Snow had voiced in the "Two Cultures" decades before, Ehlers suggested that it was considered acceptable not to understand the second law of thermodynamics, but misnaming a play by Shakespeare was somehow *un*acceptable. Scientific ignorance was casually accepted, rather than corrected, because people thought science was just too hard. Ehlers recognized the need for a culture shift when it came to how people thought about science. He explained as much to his colleagues in 1997:

> When my students talked about science being difficult, I
> would say, of course it's difficult. You're learning to think in
> a different way. This is a different mode of inquiry, it's not
> the same mode of inquiry used to study certain topics in the
> humanities, for example. It is a unique way of thinking, and a
> unique way of examining and learning information about the
> world around us.[186]

Ehlers in Flight

Ehlers began flying lessons when he lived in California. It was his favorite pet hobby and something he always wanted to pursue when he retired. Unfortunately, he rarely had time to work on his flying skills, but he would manage to catch a flying lesson here and there. He also collected model planes. One of his staffers recalled, "He would go to aviation shows and they would give him thirty model planes. He said he wanted to hang them up in his office. He never did, but he would have had thirty model airplanes up there if he could."[183]

Almost all of Ehlers's science initiatives—in any context—include a push for better science education. He put education at the front of many of his legislative decisions. When President George W. Bush revealed his hopes to revitalize NASA's mission, Ehlers, as a NASA and space science enthusiast, was pleased at the president's interest. "However," Ehlers concluded in a press release, "we must temper our enthusiasm for the president's vision with the realities that face us."[187] The realities of a limited budget must temper big visions, and Ehlers ultimately worried that space exploration would take funds away from science education. He wrote, "Furthermore, if we are going to be serious about expanding NASA and its mission, we also need to be serious about expanding our math and science education programs so that we have the scientists and engineers trained to do the work that we will be asking them to do."[188]

Ehlers's interest in science education fit well within the Bush administration's overall goals to improve education in America. Ehlers supported the No Child Left Behind Act[189] and worked for initiatives for more teacher support, resources for science educators, and partnerships between the private sector and educators.[190] Many of his specific endeavors on behalf of science/math education finally culminated in the 2007 America COMPETES (Creating Opportunities to Meaningfully Promote Excellence in Technology, Education, and Science) Act.[191] Originally signed by Bush, the America COMPETES Act has continued to be reauthorized by subsequent administrations. The act addresses the numerous science-related bodies within the United States government, with special attention to improving the ways they support math and science education. Ehlers was a key leader in crafting this legislation and was specifically thanked by President Bush for his contributions.[192] Ehlers called the act "basically everything I've worked on for 12 years."[193]

CHAPTER SEVEN
Learning from Vern

Ehlers announced his retirement on February 10, 2010, shortly after his seventy-sixth birthday. "Some people stay too long," he said to the *Grand Rapids Press*. "I wanted to go out while I was still a strong leader playing a valuable role, not forced out by health or age."[194] Ehlers's constituents were grateful for those accomplishments. His final year in Congress was filled with warm thank-yous and many events commemorating his service.

Vern and Jo, 2010

The *Press* published an opinion piece titled "We Can Learn from Vern," written by Jeff Cranson the day after the announcement. Cranson had called Ehlers on his birthday, February 6, 2010, at his Grand Rapids home to interview him for this piece and learn more about his retirement. Ehlers pointed out that Jo was not in the best of health; in fact, on that particular day, they were lying low at home because she had experienced a mild heart attack. Ehlers also said he was getting tired of the flights to and from DC. Cranson suspected Ehlers's exhaustion might have come "from trying to deal with substantive policy issues in a nation's capital obsessed with the perpetual election cycle and mired in partisanship."[195] Ehlers did miss the more positive atmosphere of his early days in Congress, when members of Congress played golf or had dinner at each other's homes. "That adds a lot to the civility," admitted Ehlers. "That just doesn't happen anymore."

Cranson's article highlights Ehlers's accomplishments in Congress, which came to pass in spite of growing partisanship. Cranson ended on a personal note, stating,

> There are many lessons in Vern's service for [those] . . . who
> aspire to succeed him, and this one's simple: Be the kind of
> guy who takes a media or constituent call on a Saturday morn-
> ing at home, even when you're quietly marking your birthday
> and helping your wife recover from a heart attack.[196]

Ehlers dealt honestly with people and made time for them—constituents, reporters, colleagues, and staff. People in his district and on the Hill remember his kindness. Jonathan Hirte recalled,

> Vern consistently did a good job, he cared for people. He built
> up a lot of trust and was well-respected across the aisle. When
> I meet people who remember Vern, they always have incredi-
> ble things to say about him. He has had a lasting impact.[197]

For many, Ehlers's particular policy areas were far from exciting or even memorable, but the way he conducted himself and the way he ran his staff left an impression. Ehlers worked hard, arriving at his conclusions through logic. He was thoughtful and kind in an environment that can be brutal.

Another of Ehlers's staffers, Julia Jester, recalled sitting in a committee meeting with Ehlers soon after he had announced his retirement. People could be very rude and overbearing in committee hearings, but Ehlers always brought a voice of "calming reason." Jester explained,

> He was able to inject the right amount of respect for everyone in the room. He encouraged respectful engagement.
>
> I remember sitting in one such hearing, when we knew he was going to retire and thinking, everyone is going to miss him so much. He just had no desire to contribute at all to that sort of negative behavior.[198]

On his retirement, many members of the press and his home district commented that Ehlers was the last of a dying breed—a measured, educated, fair-minded, and compassionate public servant who was there to really serve. This sort of attitude was becoming scarcer on the Hill. It was a rare politician who was able to talk to members of the other party with mutual respect and civility, or whose constituents—even his ideological opponents—still believed in his genuine goodness as a person.

Ehlers giving a speech in the House, 1998

Vernon J. Ehlers Amtrak Station

As a congressman, Ehlers earmarked funds to be used in the Grand Rapids public transportation system. Three years after his retirement, the new Grand Rapids Amtrak Station was named in his honor. Ehlers was unable to attend the opening ceremony on October 27, 2014, so Marla Ehlers represented the family. Local dignitaries were warm in their appreciation for Ehlers's work for the district from his position on the House Transportation committee. US Senator Carl Levin (D-MI) remarked on Ehlers's good understanding of the needs within his district and his spirit of cooperation. As the local news reported, "Ehlers brought no 'I' nor selfishness to the job, Levin said, only 'we.'"[199]

Unlike some public figures, Ehlers's kindness did not vary between his private and personal life. While the praise from his staffers and colleagues for his professional achievements and conduct is meaningful, perhaps even more telling are his private conduct and relationships. In 1966, Ehlers struck up an unusual teacher student relationship with a young man named Lyle Barber, a twenty-five-year-old inmate at the Michigan state prison in Jackson. During his incarceration for armed robbery, Barber reached out to the Berkeley physics faculty to ask for someone to help him learn physics. Ehlers agreed to work with Barber, but it was a busy chapter in his life. He and Jo were in the middle of moving their young family cross-country, and Ehlers still had responsibilities at Berkeley. But he found the time to write Barber many long letters. He set out a course for Barber to follow, helped him through difficult equations, and offered advice about how to study. Ehlers specifically encouraged him to enroll at Calvin College or Grand Valley State College to study physics. Always thorough, he tried sending Barber a *Science* magazine subscription in prison to supplement his physics education.

Letters between the two wandered into personal concerns too. Barber wrote about his life in prison; Ehlers offered anecdotes from his past. Eventually, Barber asked Ehlers to write to his parole officer, vouching for his character (which

Ehlers did), also promising that he would speak to the parole board in prison on Barber's behalf. It doesn't look like Ehlers was ever called on to support Barber in this way. But regardless, Barber was very grateful; he sent Ehlers a billfold that he had made. Ehlers was touched: "It is a beautiful piece of work," he wrote Barber on July 11, 1966, "so beautiful I hardly dare use it!"[200] In the same letter, Ehlers then promises to do as much as he can to help Barber get into a college upon his release. After Ehlers and Jo moved to Michigan later that summer, they did visit Barber in the prison on one occasion.

It is not clear that Ehlers ever spoke to anyone about Barber, except for Jo. However, he did stay in touch with Barber at least through the mid '70s.[201] When Jo recalled her husband's correspondence with Barber, she quickly responded, "That's his [Vern's] whole nature—when people needed help, and, he knew he could help them, he would."[202] Without fuss or fanfare, Ehlers got down to business helping people out of his thoughtfulness, sense of duty, and considerable talent.

Ehlers's answer as to why he went into politics was similarly straightforward: he served "out of a religious conviction of a responsibility to God and the world around us that we must care for the world and its inhabitants."[203] Ehlers found his niche in public service where the world's deep need and his deep passions met.[204] He used his scientific and administrative acumen to leave the world better than he found it and teach others how to do the same.

The Honorable Vernon J. Ehlers, 2010

APPENDIX 1
Photos used in this book

Introduction

Figure 1   Vern Ehlers, 1974
Ehlers, Courtesy of Vernon J. Ehlers Collection (Coll. 525), Heritage Hall, Hekman Library, Calvin College.

Figure 2   County Commissioner campaign pamphlet, 1974
Ehlers, Courtesy of Vernon J. Ehlers Collection (Coll. 525), Heritage Hall, Hekman Library, Calvin College.

Figure 3   Vern and children hand out spruce trees during the 1974 primary campaign for the Kent County Board of Commissioners.
Courtesy of Vernon J. Ehlers family.

Figure 4   Vern and Jo, President George W. Bush and First Lady Laura Bush, Dec 3 2001.
Ehlers served under Clinton, Bush, and Obama terms.
Ehlers, Courtesy of Vernon J. Ehlers Collection (Coll. 525), Heritage Hall, Hekman Library, Calvin College.

Chapter 1

Figure 1   Ehlers age four
Ehlers, Courtesy of Vernon J. Ehlers Collection (Coll. 525), Heritage Hall, Hekman Library, Calvin College.

Figure 2   Sam Bosch, Vern, and fellow goaters
Courtesy of Sam Bosch and the Vernon J. Ehlers Family.

Figure 3   Original caption: "Dr. Vernon J. Ehlers and Thomas Fowler operating the atomic beam magnetic-resonance apparatus at the University of California at Berkeley. Dr. Ehlers used the equipment last summer to measure the nuclear magnetic moment of Rb^{85}, and also to determine the atomic magnetic moment of Gallium."
Ehlers, Courtesy of Vernon J. Ehlers Collection (Coll. 525), Heritage Hall, Hekman Library, Calvin College.

Figure 4   Mr. & Mrs. Ehlers, June 14, 1958
Courtesy of Vernon J. Ehlers family.

Figure 5   Ehlers family, 1972
Courtesy of Vernon J. Ehlers family.

Figure 6   State Representative Paul Henry and Kent County Board of
Commissioners Chairman Vernon Ehlers, from "The Calvin
Connection: Making Room for Politics," *West Michigan Magazine*,
December 1980
Ehlers, Courtesy of Vernon J. Ehlers Collection (Coll. 525), Heritage
Hall, Hekman Library, Calvin College.

Chapter 2

Figure 1   Ehlers with physics students at Calvin, late '60s/early '70s
Ehlers, Courtesy of Vernon J. Ehlers Collection (Coll. 525), Heritage
Hall, Hekman Library, Calvin College.

Figure 2   Letter from Gerald R. Ford to Vernon Ehlers about forming a science
advisory committee, March 2, 1972
Ehlers, Courtesy of Vernon J. Ehlers Collection (Coll. 525), Heritage
Hall, Hekman Library, Calvin College.

Figure 3   Ford and Ehlers, undated
Ehlers, Courtesy of Vernon J. Ehlers Collection (Coll. 525), Heritage
Hall, Hekman Library, Calvin College.

Figure 4   Vern and volunteers celebrate his first victory, Kent County
Commission primary, 1974.
Courtesy of the Vernon J. Ehlers family.

Figure 5   A newsletter from Vern supporting recycling efforts in Kent County
Courtesy of Vernon J. Ehlers family.

Figure 6   Ehlers in State House ca. 1983–85
Ehlers, Courtesy of Vernon J. Ehlers Collection (Coll. 525), Heritage
Hall, Hekman Library, Calvin College.

Figure 7   Artist's depiction of the choice voters faced between Ehlers and
Monsma in the 1985 State Senate race
Jim Harger, "State Senate Showdown," Grand Rapids Press, March 24,
1985, A1. Microfilm, Grand Rapids History and Special Collections,
Grand Rapids Public Library.

Chapter 3

Chapter 4

Chapter 5

Figure 1   *Unlocking our Future: Toward a New National Science Policy*
Cover, 1998
Ehlers, Courtesy of Vernon J. Ehlers Collection (Coll. 525), Heritage
Hall, Hekman Library, Calvin College.

Figure 2   Ehlers accepts certificated naming him a fellow from the American
Physical Society from the APS president, Dr. Kumar Patel. October 18,
1995.
Ehlers, Courtesy of Vernon J. Ehlers Collection (Coll. 525), Heritage
Hall, Hekman Library, Calvin College.

Figure 3   Ehlers's drawing illustrating "The Valley of Death"
Ehlers, Courtesy of Vernon J. Ehlers Collection (Coll. 525), Heritage
Hall, Hekman Library, Calvin College.

Chapter 6

Figure 1   Ehlers with a different NASA crew, Shuttle mission crew STS-108,
2001
Ehlers, Courtesy of Vernon J. Ehlers Collection (Coll. 525), Heritage
Hall, Hekman Library, Calvin College.

Figure 2   Ehlers with staff ca. 2005: Bill McBride, Leslee Rohs, Kelli Scholten,
Julia Jester, Kevan Chapman, Rachel Fenton, Matt Reiffer, Vern, Ben
Gielow, Jenny Ungrey, Matt Evans, Rick Treur, Jennifer Duthler, Jeremy
Dalpiaz
Courtesy of the Vernon J. Ehlers family.

Figure 3   Ehlers would often wear a Cat in the Hat hat when he visited schools
to read to children.
Ehlers, Courtesy of Vernon J. Ehlers Collection (Coll. 525), Heritage
Hall, Hekman Library, Calvin College.

Figure 4   Dr. Ehlers teaching a demonstration class, late '60s/early '70s
Ehlers, Courtesy of Vernon J. Ehlers Collection (Coll. 525), Heritage
Hall, Hekman Library, Calvin College.

Chapter 7

APPENDIX 2
Vernon J. Ehlers Publications

Physics Bibliography, 1959–1973

"Nuclear Spin, Hyperfine Structure Separation and Magnetic Moment of 220hr Potassium-43," with F. R. Petersen, W. B. Ewbank, L. L. Marino, and H. A. Shugart, *Physics Review* 116, 734 (1959).

"Hyperfine-Structure Separation and Nuclear Moments Gallium-68," with H. A. Shugart, *Physics Review* 127, 529 (1962).

"Nuclear Spin of Gallium-70," with W. A. Nierenberg and H. A. Shugart, *Physics Review* 125, 2008 (1962).

"Hyperfine-Structure Separation, Nuclear Magnetic Moment, and Hyperfine-Structure Anomaly of Cesium-131," with Richard D. Worley, William A. Nierenberg, and Howard A. Shugart, *Physics Review* 140, 1483 (1965).

"Nuclear Spin and Magnetic Dipole Moment of 39-Min Au-190," with Yau Wa Chan and William Nierenberg, *Physics Review* 144, 1020 (1966).

"Nuclear Magnetic Movement, Hyperfine Structure, and Hyperfine-Structure Anomaly of Ag^{110m}," with Stephen C. Schmelling and Howard A. Shugart, *Physics Review* 154, 1142 (1967).

"Hyperfine Structure Measurements on Dy^{161} and Dy^{163}," with W. Ebenhoh and J. Ferch, *Zeitschrift für Physik* 200, 84 (1967).

"Hyperfine-Structure Separations, Nuclear Magnetic Moments, and Hyperfine-Structure

Anomalies of Gold-198 and Gold-199," with Paul A. Vanden Bout, William A. Nierenberg, and Howard A. Shugart, *Physics Review* 158, 1078 (1967).

"Precision Measurement of the Electronic g Factors of the Alkali Metals," with Paul A. Vanden Bout, Erol Aygun, Tuncay Incesu, Adman Saplakiglu, and Howard A. Shugart, *Physics Reviews* 165, 88 (1968).

"Nuclear Spin, Hyperfine-Structure Separation, and Nuclear Magnetic Moment of 18-min Rb^{88}," with Paul A. Vanden Bout, Antoni Dymanus, Michael H. Prior, and Howard A. Shugart, *Physics Review* 166, 1131 (1968).

"Nuclear Magnetic Moment of Rb^{85}: Resolving a Discrepancy," with Thomas R. Fowler and Howard A. Shugart, *Physics Review* 167, 1062 (1968).

"Hyperfine Structure of ^{67}Ga and ^{72}Ga," with Yurdanus Kabasakal, Howard A. Shugart, and Orhan Tezer, *Physics Review* 176, 25 (1968).

"Nuclear Magnetic Moment, Hyperfine Structure, and Hyperfine-Structure Anomaly of ^{196}Au," with Stephen G. Schmelling and Howard A. Shugart, *Physics Review* C2, 225 (1970).

"Search for an Electron Shift in ^{133}Cs in an Intense Electromagnetic Field," with J. Richard Mowat, Charles E. Johnson, and Howard A. Shugart, *Physics Review* D3, 43 (1971).

"Electron Excitation of the Calcium 4227-A Resonance Line," with Alan Gallagher, *Physics Review* A7, 1573 (1973).

"A Reliable, Repetitively Pulsed, High-Power Nitrogen Laser," with Benjamin Woodward and Lineberger, *Review of Scientific Instruments* 44, 883 (1973).

"Science Faculty Fellowship #61065 Final Report," (1973).

Science, Religion, and Stewardship, 1969–1998

Ehlers, Vernon J.; Griffioen, R. C., "The Christian and Science: a Symposium": Grand Rapids, Calvin College 1969.

Triezenberg, Henry, J; Ehlers, Vernon J. *Readings in Science Education,* Grand Rapids Michigan: National Union of Christian Schools, 1970.

Task Force on World Hunger; Paul G. Schrotenboer, chair, *And He Had Compassion on Them : The Christian and World Hunger: Prepared for the Christian Reformed Church Synod.* Grand Rapids: Education Department of the CRC, 1978.

Task Force on World Hunger; Paul G. Schrotenboer, chair, *For My Neighbor's Good: World Hunger and Structural Change.* Grand Rapids: Board of Publications of the Christian Reformed Church, 1979.

Wilkinson, Loren; De Vos, Peter; Dykema, Eugene; Ehlers, Vernon J.; De Wiit, Calvin, *Earthkeeping: Christian stewardship of natural resources.* Grand Rapids: William B. Eerdmans Publishing Company, 1980.

DeWitt, Calvin B.; Baer, Richard A.; Derr, Thomas Sieger, and others, *Caring for Creation: Responsible Stewardship of God's Handiwork.* Grand Rapids: Baker Books, 1998.

Other Publications, 1985–2001

Ehlers, Vernon J. *A Student's Guide to College Admission and Financial Aid.* [Lansing: Michigan Senate] 1985.

Ehlers, Vernon J. "Computer Viruses: Attacking Computer Crime with Legislation." [Lansing] : Michigan Legislative Service Bureau, Science and Technology Division, 1989.

Ehlers, Vernon J; Muzika, Rose-Marie; Gales, Julie. *The US Constitution and You,* [Lansing?]: Science and Technology Division, Legislative Service Bureau, 1990.

Muzika, Rose-Marie, 1958-; Gales, Julie.; Ehlers, Vernon J. *Trees and Air: Local Action on Global Problems,* [Lansing?]: Science and Technology Division, Legislative Service Bureau, 1990.

Constituent Guides Provided by State Senator Ehlers, [Lansing].
1. *"A Student's Guide to State Government,"*
2. *"Citizens Guide to State Government: Provided* (revised/updated 1993),
3. *"The Legislative Process in Michigan: A Student's Guide—Provided* (April 1993)

Ehlers, Vernon J ; Smith, Howard K. *The US Constitution and You,* Washington, DC: Distributed by the Committee for Citizen Awareness, 1994. Video.

Ehlers, Vernon J; Manatos, Andrew E; *Your Executive Branch and You,* Washington, DC: Distributed by the Committee for Citizen Awareness, 1995. Video.

Ehlers, Vernon J. *A Physicist in Congress a Clash of Cultures,* 1997. Video.

Ehlers, Vernon J. "Information Warfare and International Security," Brussels: NATO Parliamentary Assembly, International Secretariat, 1999.

Ehlers, Vernon J. *Your Executive Branch and You,* Washington, DC: Distributed by the Committee for Citizen Awareness, 1999. Video.

Ehlers, Vernon J. *Where we Stand Democracy, free enterprise, and our standard of living* Washington, DC: Distributed by the Committee for Citizen Awareness, 2000. Video.

Ehlers, Vernon J; Kennedy, Caroline. *We the People—The US Constitution and You,* Washington, DC: Distributed by the Committee for Citizen Awareness, 2001. Video.

APPENDIX 3
Congressional Committees

Committee on Education and Labor
    Subcommittee on Early Childhood, Elementary and Secondary Education
    Subcommittee on Higher Education, Lifelong Learning, and Competitiveness
Committee on Science and Technology
    Subcommittee on Energy and Environment
    Subcommittee on Research and Science Education (Ranking Member)
Committee on Transportation and Infrastructure
    Subcommittee on Aviation
    Subcommittee on Coast Guard and Maritime Transportation
    Subcommittee on Water Resources and Environment
Committee on House Administration (Ranking Member)
Committee on Education and the Workforce
    Subcommittee on 21st-Century Competitiveness
    Subcommittee on Education Reform
Committee on Science
    Subcommittee on Energy
    Subcommittee on Environment Technology and Standards (Chair)
Joint Committee on the Library of Congress

NOTES

Introduction

1   Vernon J. Ehlers, "A Physicist in County Government" *American Institute of Physics* 1978 Section E: Specific Public Sector Career Experiences 239-242 Box 15, Folder 8. Ehlers Vernon J. Collection # 525. Heritage Hall Calvin College Archives.

2   Scot Christenson, "Creating a Better Curriculum: A Ripon Interview with U.S. Representative Vernon Ehlers (R-MI)." *Ripon Forum*. April 2002, 5. Box 12, Folder 23, Ehlers Vernon J. Collection # 525. Heritage Hall Calvin College Archives.

3   Scot Christenson, "Creating a Better Curriculum: A Ripon Interview with U.S. Representative Vernon Ehlers (R-MI)." *Ripon Forum*. April 2002, 5. Box 12, Folder 23, Ehlers Vernon J. Collection # 525. Heritage Hall Calvin College Archives.

Chapter 1

4   Ted Roelofs, "A Hectic Pace" *Grand Rapids Press: Perspectives*, June 5, 1994, F1. Box 54, Folder 2, Ehlers Vernon J. Collection # 525. Heritage Hall Calvin College Archives.

5   Ehlers was approached by a handful of academic institutions about administrative positions.

6   The Ehlerses immigrated from the Netherlands, but the family name actually originated in northern Germany.

7   Information about the Ehlers family history has been provided by Marla Ehlers and Heidi Rienstra (née Ehlers).

8   Michael Cox, "Vern Ehlers: Square Shooter," *Grand Rapids Press: Wonderland Section*, June 23, 1985, Box 24 folder 4, Ehlers Vernon J. Collection # 525. Heritage Hall Calvin College Archives.

9   Hennie Buurma (Ehlers's sister) interview with the author, July 24, 2017.

10   Ted Roelofs, "A Hectic Pace" *Grand Rapids Press: Perspectives*, June 5, 1994, F1. Box 54, Folder 2, Ehlers Vernon J. Collection # 525. Heritage Hall Calvin College Archives.

11   Michael Cox, "Vern Ehlers: Square Shooter," *Grand Rapids Press: Wonderland Section*, June 23, 1985, Box 24 folder 4, Ehlers Vernon J. Collection # 525. Heritage Hall Calvin College Archives.

12   Vernon Ehlers, interview by John Norton Smith, July 21, 2010, *Gerald R. Ford Oral History Project*. http://geraldrfordfoundation.org/centennial/oralhistory/vern-ehlers/.

13   Physics notes courtesy of Matthew Walhout.

14   Jo Ehlers, (Vernon Ehlers's wife) in discussion with the author, July 7, 2017.

15 "Ehlers Brings a Physicist's Perspective to Capitol Hill," *American Physical Society News* 3, no 9 (1994): 2. Personal Papers of Roger Griffioen Professor of Physics Emeritus Calvin College.

16 Jo Ehlers, (Vernon Ehlers's wife) in discussion with the author, July 7, 2017.

17 Vernon J. Ehlers to Dr. Peter Boelens, October 17, 1979, Personal Papers of Vernon Ehlers [file E].

18 Vernon Ehlers, interview by John Norton Smith, July 21, 2010, *Gerald R. Ford Oral History Project*. http://geraldrfordfoundation.org/centennial/oralhistory/vern-ehlers/.

19 Vernon Ehlers, interview by John Norton Smith, July 21, 2010, *Gerald R. Ford Oral History Project*. http://geraldrfordfoundation.org/centennial/oralhistory/vern-ehlers/.

20 Dennis Hoekstra (Friend of Ehlers, member of Eastern Avenue CRC, retired Calvin College faculty member, activist) in discussion with the author, July 2016.

21 Bill McBride (Ehlers's Chief of Staff), interview with the author, July 21, 2017.

22 Marg Ed Conn. "The Calvin Connection: Making Room for Politics," *West Michigan Magazine*, December 1980, 28. Box 67, Folder 8. Ehlers Vernon J. Collection # 525. Heritage Hall Calvin College Archives.

23 Marg Ed Conn. "The Calvin Connection: Making Room for Politics," *West Michigan Magazine*, December 1980, 27. Box 67, Folder 8. Ehlers Vernon J. Collection # 525. Heritage Hall Calvin College Archives.

24 Jim Harger, "Calvin: College of Candidates," *Grand Rapids Press*, January 13, 1985, Box 24 folder 4. Ehlers Vernon J. Collection # 525. Heritage Hall Calvin College Archives.

25 Jim Harger, "Calvin: College of Candidates," *Grand Rapids Press*, January 13, 1985, Box 24 folder 4. Ehlers Vernon J. Collection # 525. Heritage Hall Calvin College Archives.

26 Vernon J. Ehlers, (draft) "Protecting and Enhancing Life" (October 13, 2003), (speech, Kuyper Institute Lecture for Center for Public Justice, Grand Rapids, MI). Box 40, Folder 29. Ehlers Vernon J. Collection # 525. Heritage Hall Calvin College Archives.

27 Vernon J. Ehlers to Mr. and Mrs. James E. McKay, September 24, 1993, Unprocessed Archive. Heritage Hall Calvin College Archives.

28 "Candidate profiles: 3rd Congressional District" Tuesday October 29, 2002 Mlive.com Tuesday October 29, 2002, Box 17 Folder 5, Ehlers Vernon J. Collection # 525. Heritage Hall Calvin College Archives.

29 Rick Treur (Ehlers's district services manager) interview with the author, June 24, 2016.

30   Vernon Ehlers, interview by John Norton Smith, July 21, 2010, *Gerald R. Ford Oral History Project*. http://geraldrfordfoundation.org/centennial/oralhistory/vern-ehlers/.

31   Vernon Ehlers, "Everything I Really Needed to Know I Learned too Late!" (speech, Michigan State University Commencement, East Lansing, MI, May 8, 1998). Box 41, Folder 61. Ehlers Vernon J. Collection # 525. Heritage Hall Calvin College Archives.

32   Vernon J. Ehlers. "Challenges for Undergraduate Science Education," Research and Excellence at Undergraduate Institutions: Annual Report (2000), 17, Box 67, Folder 36, Ehlers Vernon J. Collection # 525. Heritage Hall Calvin College Archives.

       Stephen J. Norton, "Congress—Act of God:" *National Journal*, March 18, 2000, https://www.nationaljournal.com/s/606358/congress-act-god?mref=search-result

       State of Michigan Special Tribute," December 22, 1993, Box 23 Folder 6, Collection # 525 Ehlers, Vernon J. Heritage Hall, Calvin College Archives.

Chapter 2

33   Vernon J Ehlers to Roger Griffioen, November 10, 1965, Box 16, folder 3, Ehlers Vernon J. Collection # 525. Heritage Hall Calvin College Archives.

34   Roger Griffioen, interview with the author, June 2016.

35   Roger Griffioen, interview with the author, June 2016.

36   Dennis Hoekstra (Friend of Ehlers, member of Eastern Avenue CRC, retired Calvin College faculty member, activist) in discussion with the author, July 2016.

37   Roger Griffioen to Dr. Bruce Miller, Executive Director Presidential Search Committee Michigan State University, July 9, 1993. Personal Papers Roger Griffioen, Professor of Physics Emeritus Calvin College.

38   Vernon J. Ehlers to William Spoelhof, President of Calvin College, November 4, 1965, Box 16 folder 2, Ehlers Vernon J. Collection # 525. Heritage Hall Calvin College Archives.

39   Vernon Ehlers, interview by John Norton Smith, July 21, 2010, *Gerald R. Ford Oral History Project*. http://geraldrfordfoundation.org/centennial/oralhistory/vern-ehlers/.

40   To R. D. Griffieon from V. Ehlers. Memo. "Time of Lack Thereof," 25, November 1968. Personal Papers Roger Griffioen, Professor of Physics Emeritus Calvin College.

41   Marla Ehlers, (Vernon Ehlers's daughter) in discussion with the author, July 18, 2016.

42   Roger Griffioen, interview with the author, June 2016.

43   Irwin Goodwin, "At last a physicist active in APS elected to House" *Physics Today* (January 1994), 37, Box 54, Folder 1, Ehlers Vernon J. Collection # 525. Heritage Hall Calvin College Archives.

44   Calvin College News Release, December 18, 1970. Box 17 Folder 8, Ehlers Vernon J. Collection # 525. Heritage Hall Calvin College Archives.

45   "McCormack, Mike," Biographical Directory of the United States, August 2, 2016, Congress http://bioguide.congress.gov/scripts/biodisplay.pl?index=M000365.

46   "Ford Science Advice," *Science Trends* 32, no. 20 (August 26, 1974): 155, Personal Papers of Vernon J. Ehlers.

47   "Mr Ford and Science Policy," *Science* 185, no. 4152 (August 23, 1974), Personal Papers of Vernon J. Ehlers.

48   "Mr Ford and Science Policy," *Science* 185, no. 4152 (August 23, 1974), Personal Papers of Vernon J. Ehlers.

49   Vernon J Ehlers. "A Physicist in County Government" *American Institute of Physics* 1978 Section E: Specific Public Sector Career Experiences 239-242 Box 15, Folder 8. Ehlers Vernon J. Collection # 525. Heritage Hall Calvin College Archives.

50   Vernon J Ehlers. "A Physicist in County Government" *American Institute of Physics* 1978 Section E: Specific Public Sector Career Experiences 239-242 Box 15, Folder 8. Ehlers Vernon J. Collection # 525. Heritage Hall Calvin College Archives.

51   "Primary Results at a Glance" *Grand Rapids Press*, August 7, 1974. Grand Rapids History and Special Collections, Grand Rapids Public Library.

52   Vernon J. Ehlers. "Memoirs of a County Commissioner." unpublished article. February 1982. Box 18, Folder 16, Ehlers Vernon J. Collection # 525. Heritage Hall Calvin College Archives.

53   Vernon J Ehlers. "A Physicist in County Government" *American Institute of Physics* 1978 Section E: Specific Public Sector Career Experiences 239-242 Box 15, Folder 8. Ehlers Vernon J. Collection # 525. Heritage Hall Calvin College Archives.

54   "Vern Ehlers for Republican State Representative," pamphlet, 1982. Box 19 Folder 2, Ehlers, Vernon J. Collection # 525. Heritage Hall Calvin College Archives.

55   Vernon J. Ehlers. "A Brief History of Recycling in Kent County." February 10, 1982. Box 18 Folder 17, Ehlers, Vernon J. Collection # 525. Heritage Hall Calvin College Archives.

56   Beth Bandstra (Ehlers's county commissioner campaign manager, district services manager 1993-97, and friend from Eastern Avenue CRC), interview with the author, August 10, 2016.

57   "Vernon J Ehlers for State Representative" Campaign Flyer. Box 19, Folder 2, Ehlers, Vernon J. Collection # 525. Heritage Hall Calvin College Archives.

58   Ehlers to run for 93rd House Seat" *Grand Rapids Press*. Box. 19, Folder 2, Ehlers, Vernon J. Collection # 525. Heritage Hall Calvin College Archives.

59   Marla Ehlers (Vernon Ehlers's daughter), in discussion with the author, July 18, 2016.

60   Milton Coleman, "Democrats Aim At Upset in Michigan Race," *The Washington Post*, March 25, 1985, A3. Box 20 Folder 1, Ehlers, Vernon J. Collection # 525. Heritage Hall Calvin College Archives.

61   Milton Coleman, "Democrats Aim At Upset in Michigan Race," *The Washington Post*, March 25, 1985, A3. Box 20 Folder 1, Ehlers, Vernon J. Collection # 525. Heritage Hall Calvin College Archives.

62   Milton Coleman, "Democrats Aim At Upset in Michigan Race," *The Washington Post*, March 25, 1985, A3. Box 20 Folder 1, Ehlers, Vernon J. Collection # 525. Heritage Hall Calvin College Archives.

63   Vernon Ehlers State Representative Office to "Dear Future Colleagues," November 8, 1984. Box 22, folder 6, Collection # 525 Ehlers, Vernon J. Heritage Hall, Calvin College Archives.

64   From office of Vernon Ehlers Republican State Representative to Reverend and Mrs. James Dekker, December 21, 1984. Box 22, folder 1, Collection # 525 Ehlers, Vernon J. Heritage Hall, Calvin College Archives.

65   Becky Maatman. "Campaigning in Love: Brothers in Christ Oppose Each Other in Election." *Banner*, March 18, 1985, 24. Box 20, folder 11, Collection # 525 Ehlers, Vernon J. Heritage Hall, Calvin College Archives.

66   Becky Maatman. "Campaigning in Love: Brothers in Christ Oppose Each Other in Election." *Banner*, March 18, 1985, 24. Box 20, folder 11, Collection # 525 Ehlers, Vernon J. Heritage Hall, Calvin College Archives.

67   Ed Hoogterp. "Ehlers, Monsma Find Differences." *Grand Rapids Press*, March 12, 1985, 81. Box 22, Folder 6, Collection # 525 Ehlers, Vernon J. Heritage Hall, Calvin College Archives.

68   "50th Anniversary 1965-2015 Michigan Newborn Screening: A Public Health Success Story, *Michigan Department of Health & Human Services*, http://www.michigan.gov/documents/mdch/Newborn_Screening_Book_500007_7.pdf.

69   Stephen J. Norton, "Congress—Act of God:" *National Journal*, March 18, 2000, https://www.nationaljournal.com/s/606358/congress-act-god?mref=search-result.

70   "State of Michigan Special Tribute," December 22, 1993, Box 23 Folder 6, Collection # 525 Ehlers, Vernon J. Heritage Hall, Calvin College Archives.

Chapter 3

71   John Solomon, "Invasion of the PhD's: How the Ivory Tower is Changing Capitol Hill," *The Washington Post*, October 29, 1995, C1. Box 13, Folder 9, Ehlers Vernon J. Collection # 525. Heritage Hall Calvin College Archives.

72   John Solomon, "Invasion of the PhD's: How the Ivory Tower is Changing Capitol Hill," *The Washington Post*, October 29, 1995, C1. Box 13, Folder 9, Ehlers Vernon J. Collection # 525. Heritage Hall Calvin College Archives.

73   Jo Ehlers (Vernon Ehlers's wife), in discussion with the author, July 7, 2017.

74   Jo Ehlers (Vernon Ehlers's wife), in discussion with the author, July 7, 2017.

75   Ted Roelofs "Ehlers follows easy road to Congress," *Grand Rapids Press*, December 8, 1993, Box 24, Folder 4, Ehlers Vernon J. Collection # 525. Heritage Hall Calvin College Archives.

76   https://www.youtube.com/watch?v=UzVwlORWtzQ.

77   Ted Roelofs "Winning Ehlers says voters looking for substance," *Grand Rapids Press*, November 3, 1993, Box 24, Folder 4, Ehlers Vernon J. Collection # 525. Heritage Hall Calvin College Archives.

78   Marla Ehlers (Vernon Ehlers's daughter), in discussion with the author, July 18, 2016.

79   "Ehlers Brings a Physicist's Perspective to Capitol Hill," *American Physical Society News* 3, no 9 (1994): 2. Personal Papers of Roger Griffioen Professor of Physics Emeritus Calvin College.

80   Bill McBride (Ehlers's Chief of Staff), interview with the author, July 21, 2017.

81   "Ehlers Brings a Physicist's Perspective to Capitol Hill," *American Physical Society News* 3, no 9 (1994): 6. Personal Papers of Roger Griffioen Professor of Physics Emeritus Calvin College.

82   Vernon J. Ehlers, ""Up in Michigan: Lessons for Becoming a Majority," Catalyst: *Journal of Professional Development*, no 1 (Spring 1994): 3-7. Box 67, Folder 12, Ehlers Vernon J. Collection # 525. Heritage Hall Calvin College Archives.

83   Vernon J. Ehlers, ""Up in Michigan: Lessons for Becoming a Majority," *Catalyst: Journal of Professional Development*, no 1 (Spring 1994): 3-7. Box 67, Folder 12, Ehlers Vernon J. Collection # 525. Heritage Hall Calvin College Archives.

84   Scot Christenson. "Creating a Better Curriculum: A Ripon Interview with U.S. Representative Vernon Ehlers (R-MI)." *Ripon Forum*. April 2002, 5. Box 67, Folder 38, Ehlers Vernon J. Collection # 525. Heritage Hall Calvin College Archives.

85   Scot Christenson. "Creating a Better Curriculum: A Ripon Interview with U.S. Representative Vernon Ehlers (R-MI)." *Ripon Forum*. April 2002, 5. Box 67, Folder 38, Ehlers Vernon J. Collection # 525. Heritage Hall Calvin College Archives.

86   Andrea Stone, "Decision times arrives for four on the fence" *USA Today*, October 11, 2002 10A. Box 37, Folder 56, Ehlers Vernon J. Collection # 525. Heritage Hall Calvin College Archives.

87   Andrea Stone, "Decision times arrives for four on the fence" *USA Today*, October 11, 2002 10A. Box 37, Folder 56, Ehlers Vernon J. Collection # 525. Heritage Hall Calvin College Archives.

88   Vernon J. Ehlers to President George W. Bush, September 27, 2002, Box 34, Folder 15, Ehlers Vernon J. Collection # 525. Heritage Hall Calvin College Archives.

89   Vernon J. Ehlers to President George W. Bush, September 27, 2002, Box 34, Folder 15, Ehlers Vernon J. Collection # 525. Heritage Hall Calvin College Archives.

90   Andrea Stone, "Decision times arrives for four on the fence" *USA Today*, October 11, 2002 10A. Box 37, Folder 56, Ehlers Vernon J. Collection # 525. Heritage Hall Calvin College Archives.

91   Vernon J. Ehlers, "We Can't Wait for Iraq to Strike First," *Grand Rapids Press*, October 11, 2002, A13, 1. Microfilm, Grand Rapids History and Special Collections, Grand Rapids Public Library.

92   Vernon J. Ehlers, "Statement of Congressman Vernon J. Ehlers: 'An Excruciating Moral Dilemma,'" October 10, 2002. Box 39, Folder 21, Ehlers Vernon J. Collection # 525. Heritage Hall Calvin College Archives.

93   John Agar, "Protest arrives at Ehlers's door," *Grand Rapids Press*, March 18, 2007. Box 62, Folder 7, Ehlers Vernon J. Collection # 525. Heritage Hall Calvin College Archives.

94   Vernon J Ehlers. "Floor statement Congressman Vernon J. Ehlers on H.Con.Res 63" (Congressional statement, House of Representatives, February 15, 2007). Box 34, Folder 13, Ehlers Vernon J. Collection # 525. Heritage Hall Calvin College Archives.

95   Vernon J Ehlers. "Floor statement Congressman Vernon J. Ehlers on H.Con.Res 63" (Congressional statement, House of Representatives, February 15, 2007). Box 34, Folder 13, Ehlers Vernon J. Collection # 525. Heritage Hall Calvin College Archives.

96   John Agar, "Protest arrives at Ehlers's door," *Grand Rapids Press*, March 18, 2007. Box 62, Folder 7, Ehlers Vernon J. Collection # 525. Heritage Hall Calvin College Archives.

97   Jeremy Dalpiaz (former staffer from Vernon Ehlers's Washington office), in discussion with the author, June 11, 2017.

98   Jeremy Dalpiaz (former staffer from Vernon Ehlers's Washington office), in discussion with the author, June 11, 2017.

99   Rep. Vernon Ehlers, Guest Column, "Financial rescue plan helps Main Street," *Grand Rapids Press*, October 8, 2008, A13, Ehlers Vernon J. Collection # 525. Heritage Hall Calvin College Archives.

100   Rep. Vernon Ehlers, Guest Column, "Financial rescue plan helps Main Street," *Grand Rapids Press*, October 8, 2008, A13, Ehlers Vernon J. Collection # 525. Heritage Hall Calvin College Archives.

101   Jeremy Dalpiaz (former staffer from Vernon Ehlers's Washington office), in discussion with the author, June 11, 2017.

102   "Fox News 17: Vern Ehlers Responds to Anti-war Protest," YouTube Video, 2:31, newscast March 23, 2007, posted by mediamouse, August 2, 2016, https://www.youtube.com/watch?v=3fANG2uFPlg.

Chapter 4

103   Vernon J. Ehlers, "The Jock, the Nerd, and the Whale," (speech, Calvin College commencement, Grand Rapids, MI, May 21, 1994), Box 25, Folder 33, Ehlers Vernon J. Collection # 525. Heritage Hall Calvin College Archives.

104   Vernon J. Ehlers, "The Jock, the Nerd, and the Whale," (speech, Calvin College commencement, Grand Rapids, MI, May 21, 1994), Box 25, Folder 33, Ehlers Vernon J. Collection # 525. Heritage Hall Calvin College Archives.

105   "West Michigan Environmental Action Council: About," WMEAC, August 2, 2016, http://wmeac.org/.

106   "The History of Earth Day," Earth Day Network, August 2, 2016, http://www.earthday.org/about/the-history-of-earth-day/.

107   Vernon J. Ehlers, "A Scientist's Statement of Faith," July 31, 1996, Box 37, Folder 21, Ehlers Vernon J. Collection # 525. Heritage Hall Calvin College Archives.

108   Lucas F. Johnston, *Religion and Sustainability: Social Movements and the Politics of the Environment.* New York: Routledge, 2014, 111.

109   Lucas F. Johnston, *Religion and Sustainability: Social Movements and the Politics of the Environment.* New York: Routledge, 2014, 112.

110   Lucas F. Johnston, *Religion and Sustainability: Social Movements and the Politics of the Environment.* New York: Routledge, 2014, 111.

111   Vernon J. Ehlers. "The Energetic Christian" (lecture, The 1979-80 Lectures of the Association of Reformed Colleges, Grand Rapids, MI). Box 15, Folder 17, Ehlers Vernon J. Collection # 525. Heritage Hall Calvin College Archives.

112   Vernon J. Ehlers. "The Energetic Christian" (lecture, The 1979-80 Lectures of the Association of Reformed Colleges, Grand Rapids, MI). Box 15, Folder 17, Ehlers Vernon J. Collection # 525. Heritage Hall Calvin College Archives.

113   Vernon J. Ehlers to Roger R. Rice, September 10, 1984, Box 4, Folder 4, Ehlers Vernon J. Collection # 525. Heritage Hall Calvin College Archives.

114   "Peak oil explained by U.S. Representative Vernon Ehlers, part 1," YouTube Video, recorded lecture, June 20, 2008, posted by Local Future, July 13, 2017. https://www.youtube.com/watch?v=gSdGU3XZmLk.

115   Irwin Goodwin, "At last a physicist active in APS elected to to House" *Physics Today* (January 1994), 37, Box 54, Folder 1, Ehlers Vernon J. Collection # 525. Heritage Hall Calvin College Archives.

116   Vernon J. Ehlers Curriculum Vitae, August 8, 1980. Box 1, Folder 1, Ehlers Vernon J. Collection # 525. Heritage Hall Calvin College Archives.

117   Rick Treur (Ehlers's district services manager), interview with the author, June 24, 2016.

118   "National Environmental Scorecard: Representative Vernon Ehlers," League of Conservation Voters, August 2, 2016, http://scorecard.lcv.org/moc/vernon-j-ehlers.

119   Ed Golder "Ehlers lauded as Green Giant," *Grand Rapids Press*, June 5, 2006, Grand Rapids History and Special Collections, Grand Rapids Public Library.

120   "Great Lakes initiative weakened; Ehlers loses: His amendment calling for mandatory compliance is replaced by one more favorable to governors" *Grand Rapids Associated Press*, April 6, 1995. Box 54, Folder 5, Ehlers Vernon J. Collection # 525. Heritage Hall Calvin College Archives.

121   "Michigans' Ehlers, Upton Stand Ground for Environment," Ann Arbor News, August 3, 1995, Box 54, Folder 5, Ehlers Vernon J. Collection # 525. Heritage Hall Calvin College Archives.

122   "Michigans' Ehlers, Upton Stand Ground for Environment," Ann Arbor News, August 3, 1995, Box 54, Folder 5, Ehlers Vernon J. Collection # 525. Heritage Hall Calvin College Archives.

123   David Sanger, "In Energy Plan, Bush Urges New Drilling, Conservation and Nuclear Power Review," *New York Times*, May 17, 2001, http://www.nytimes.com/2001/05/17/politics/17POWE.html?pagewanted=all

124   Ed Golder, "Ehlers lauded as Green Giant," *Grand Rapids Press*, June 5, 2006, Grand Rapids History and Special Collections, Grand Rapids Public Library.

125   Ed Golder, "Ehlers lauded as Green Giant," Grand Rapids Press, June 5, 2006, Grand Rapids History and Special Collections, Grand Rapids Public Library.

126   "Great Lakes Advocate to Retire from Congress; Pols Weigh Ehlers' Legacy," *Great Lakes Echo*, February 11, 2010, http://greatlakesecho.org/2010/02/11/great-lakes-advocate-announces-retirement-from-congress-political-watchers-weigh-loss-of-moderate-republican/.

127   Vernon J. Ehlers, "Statement: Great Lakes Legacy Act of 2002, HR 1070," September 4, 2002, Box 39, Folder 26 Ehlers Vernon J. Collection # 525. Heritage Hall Calvin College Archives. HR 1070, Great Lakes and Lake Champlain Act of 2002, became law on November 27, 2002. The Great Lakes Legacy Reauthorization Act of 2008 (HR 6460) became law on October 8, 2008.

128   "Great Lakes Advocate to Retire from Congress; Pols Weigh Ehlers' Legacy," *Great Lakes Echo*, February 11, 2010, http://greatlakesecho.org/2010/02/11/great-lakes-advo-cate-announces-retirement-from-congress-political-watchers-weigh-loss-of-moderate-re-publican/.

129   "About the Great Lakes Legacy Act," United States Environmental Protection Agency, September 7, 2015, https://www.epa.gov/great-lakes-legacy-act/about-great-lakes-legacy-act/.

130   "About the Great Lakes Legacy Act," United States Environmental Protection Agency, September 7, 2015, https://www.epa.gov/great-lakes-legacy-act/about-great-lakes-legacy-act/.

131   Ed Golder, "Ehlers lauded as Green Giant," *Grand Rapids Press*, June 5, 2006, Grand Rapids History and Special Collections, Grand Rapids Public Library.

132   "The Case for a Presidential Science Debate," host Ira Flatow, Science Friday, *NPR*, May 11, 2012, http://www.sciencefriday.com/segments/the-case-for-a-presidential-science-debate/.

133   "Great Lakes Advocate to Retire from Congress; Pols Weigh Ehlers' Legacy," *Great Lakes Echo*, February 11, 2010, http://greatlakesecho.org/2010/02/11/great-lakes-advo-cate-announces-retirement-from-congress-political-watchers-weigh-loss-of-moderate-re-publican/.

134   Jeremy Dalpiaz, (former staffer from Vernon Ehlers's Washington office) in discussion with the author, June 11, 2017.

Chapter 5

135   Vernon J. Ehlers to Mr. Ronald K. Fisk, August 20, 1969, Box 17, Folder 1, Ehlers Vernon J. Collection #525. Heritage Hall Calvin College Archives.

136   Vernon J. Ehlers. *Unlocking Our Future: Toward a New National Science Policy*, (US Committee on Science, House of Representatives One Hundred Fifth Congress 1998): 11-12, http://www.aaas.org/sites/default/files/migrate/uploads/GPO-CPRT-105hprt105-b.pdf.

137   Vernon J. Ehlers. "Scientists, the People, and the 105th Congress" (presentation, Washington Roundtable on Science & Public Policy. George C. Marshall Institute, Washington, DC, March 10, 1997): 14, Box 19, Folder 16, Ehlers Vernon J. Collection #525. Heritage Hall Calvin College Archives.

138   "Text of Speaker Gingrich's Remarks to Science Roundtable" (October 23, 1997), Box 9, Folder 2, Ehlers Vernon J. Collection #525. Heritage Hall Calvin College Archives.

139 Vernon J. Ehlers. *Unlocking Our Future: Toward a New National Science Policy*, (US Committee on Science, House of Representatives One Hundred Fifth Congress 1998): 2, http://www.aaas.org/sites/default/files/migrate/uploads/GPO-CPRT-105hprt105-b.pdf.

140 "Text of Representative Vernon Ehlers' Remarks to Science Roundtable" (October 23, 1997), Box 9, Folder 2, Ehlers Vernon J. Collection #525. Heritage Hall Calvin College Archives.

141 "Text of Representative Vernon Ehlers' Remarks to Science Roundtable" (October 23, 1997), Box 9, Folder 2, Ehlers Vernon J. Collection #525. Heritage Hall Calvin College Archives.

142 Vernon J. Ehlers. *Unlocking Our Future: Toward a New National Science Policy*, (US Committee on Science, House of Representatives One Hundred Fifth Congress 1998): 8, http://www.aaas.org/sites/default/files/migrate/uploads/GPO-CPRT-105hprt105-b.pdf.

143 Vannevar Bush, *Science, the Endless Frontier: A Report to the President on a Program for Postwar Scientific Research* (Washington, DC: National Science Foundation, 1960): 7, http://quod.lib.umich.edu/cgi/t/text/text-idx?c=acls;cc=acls;idno=heb01131.0001.00 1;node=heb01131.0001.001%3A3;view=toc7

144 "Text of Representative Vernon Ehlers' Remarks to Science Roundtable" (October 23, 1997), Box 9, Folder 2, Ehlers Vernon J. Collection #525. Heritage Hall Calvin College Archives.

145 As quoted in: Vernon J. Ehlers. "Scientists, the People, and the 105th Congress" (presentation, Washington Roundtable on Science & Public Policy. George C. Marshall Institute, Washington, DC, March 10, 1997): 1, Box 19, Folder 16, Ehlers Vernon J. Collection #525. Heritage Hall Calvin College Archives.

146 Vernon J. Ehlers. "Scientists, the People, and the 105th Congress" (presentation, Washington Roundtable on Science & Public Policy. George C. Marshall Institute, Washington, DC, March 10, 1997): 2, Box 19, Folder 16, Ehlers Vernon J. Collection #525. Heritage Hall Calvin College Archives.

147 Vernon J. Ehlers. "Scientists, the People, and the 105th Congress" (presentation, Washington Roundtable on Science & Public Policy. George C. Marshall Institute, Washington, DC, March 10, 1997): 9, Box 19, Folder 16, Ehlers Vernon J. Collection #525. Heritage Hall Calvin College Archives.

148 Vannevar Bush, *Science, the Endless Frontier: A Report to the President on a Program for Postwar Scientific Research* (Washington, DC: National Science Foundation, 1960): 12, http://quod.lib.umich.edu/cgi/t/text/text-idx?c=acls;cc=acls;idno=heb01131.0001.0 01;node=heb01131.0001.001%3A3;view=toc

149 Vernon J. Ehlers. "Scientists, the People, and the 105th Congress" (presentation, Washington Roundtable on Science & Public Policy. George C. Marshall Institute, Washington, DC, March

10, 1997): 11, Box 19, Folder 16, Ehlers Vernon J. Collection #525. Heritage Hall Calvin College Archives.

150   Vernon J. Ehlers. *Unlocking Our Future: Toward a New National Science Policy*, (U.S. Committee on Science, House of Representatives One Hundred Fifth Congress 1998): 46, http://www.aaas.org/sites/default/files/migrate/uploads/GPO-CPRT-105hprt105-b.pdf.

151   Vernon J. Ehlers to Mr. Ronald K. Fisk, August 20, 1969, Box 17, Folder 1, Ehlers Vernon J. Collection #525. Heritage Hall Calvin College Archives.

152   Vernon J. Ehlers. *Unlocking Our Future: Toward a New National Science Policy*, (U.S. Committee on Science, House of Representatives One Hundred Fifth Congress 1998): 47, http://www.aaas.org/sites/default/files/migrate/uploads/GPO-CPRT-105hprt105-b.pdf.

153   Vernon J. Ehlers. *Unlocking Our Future: Toward a New National Science Policy*, (U.S. Committee on Science, House of Representatives One Hundred Fifth Congress 1998): 48, http://www.aaas.org/sites/default/files/migrate/uploads/GPO-CPRT-105hprt105-b.pdf.

154   Vernon J Ehlers, "The Case Against Human Cloning, " *Hofstra Law Review* l 27, Iss 3 Article 5 (1999): 524, August 2, 2016 http://scholarlycommons.law.hofstra.edu/cgi/viewcontent.cgi?article=2046&context=hlr.

155   Vernon J Ehlers, "The Case Against Human Cloning, " *Hofstra Law Review* l 27, Iss 3 Article 5 (1999): 531, August 2, 2016 http://scholarlycommons.law.hofstra.edu/cgi/viewcontent.cgi?article=2046&context=hlr.

156   Peter De Vos, Calvin De Witt, Eugene Dykema, Vernon Ehlers, Derk Pereboom, Aileen van Beilen, Loren Wilkinson, "Lecture 1 Energy, Power, and Stewardship" (Lecture, The 1979-80 Lectures of the Association of Reformed Colleges, Grand Rapids, MI): 15, Box 15, Folder 19, Ehlers Vernon J. Collection #525. Heritage Hall Calvin College Archives.

157   *Sense of House Regarding National Science Policy, House of Representatives*, H. RES. 578, 105 Cong, 2nd session, *Congressional Record* 140 (October 8, 1998): H10151.

158   *Sense of House Regarding National Science Policy, House of Representatives*, H. RES. 578, 105 Cong, 2nd session, *Congressional Record* 140 (October 8, 1998): H10150.

159   Julia Jester (DC Staffer), interview with the author, July 14, 2017.

160   Colin Macilwain, "Report to Congress 'ducks major issues,'" *Nature: International Weekly Journal of Science* 395, October 1, 1998, http://www.nature.com/nature/journal/v395/n6701/full/395421a0.html.

161   Colin Macilwain, "Report to Congress 'ducks major issues,'" *Nature: International Weekly Journal of Science* 395, October 1, 1998, http://www.nature.com/nature/journal/v395/n6701/full/395421a0.html.

162   "Text of Speaker Gingrich's Remarks to Science Roundtable" (October 23, 1997), Box 9, Folder 2, Ehlers Vernon J. Collection #525. Heritage Hall Calvin College Archives.

163   *Sense of House Regarding National Science Policy, House of Representatives*, H. RES. 578, 105 Cong, 2nd session, *Congressional Record* 140 (October 8, 1998): H10150.

164   George Brown, "Opinion: On Unlocking Our Future," *APS News* 8, no 1, (January 1999) : 4, https://www.aps.org/publications/apsnews/199901/upload/jan99.pdf.

165   *Sense of House Regarding National Science Policy, House of Representatives*, H. RES. 578, 105 Cong, 2nd session, *Congressional Record* 140 (October 8, 1998): H10154.

166   *Sense of House Regarding National Science Policy, House of Representatives*, H. RES. 578, 105 Cong, 2nd session, *Congressional Record* 140 (October 8, 1998): H10151.

167   Daniel S. Greenberg, *Science, Money, and Politics: Political Triumph and Ethical Erosion*, (University of Chicago Press: 2003), 40, Accessed August 3, 2016, https://books.google.com.

Chapter 6

168   Vernon J. Ehlers, "Guest column: Bolster Math, Science Efforts without Sputnik-like Spark," *Grand Rapids Press*, October 8, 2007, Box 19c, Folder 2, Ehlers Vernon J. Collection # 525. Heritage Hall Calvin College Archives.

169   Vernon J. Ehlers. "Challenges for Undergraduate Science Education," *Research and Excellence at Undergraduate Institutions:Annual Report* (2000), 22, Box 67, Folder 36, Ehlers Vernon J. Collection # 525. Heritage Hall Calvin College Archives.

170   Beth Bandstra (Ehlers's county commissioner campaign manager, district services manager 1993-97, and friend from Eastern Avenue CRC), interview with the author, August 10, 2016.

171   Bill McBride (Ehlers's Chief of Staff), interview with the author, July 21, 2017.

172   Jeremy Dalpiaz (former DC Staffer), in discussion with the author, June 11, 2017.

173   Rachel ten Haaf (former DC Staffer), in correspondence with the author, June 8, 2017.

174   Jonathan Hirte (DC Staffer), interview with the author, May 20, 2017.

175   Julia Jester (DC Staffer), interview with the author, July 14, 2017.

176   Ehlers Vernon J. Collection #525, Box 23 Folder 11 "State Senate Guides to Government (Constitutional Handouts), 1993, Heritage Hall Calvin College Archives. Ehlers also co-wrote similar citizen-education materials as a US congressman.

177   "Rename the Ionia City Post Office to Honor Civil War Hero Alonzo Woodruff" Dear Colleagues letter from Ehlers congressional office, Box 67, Folder 36, Ehlers Vernon J. Collection # 525. Heritage Hall Calvin College Archives.

178   Doug Koopman (professor of political science at Calvin College), interview with the author, June 27, 2016.

179 "The Case for a Presidential Science Debate," host Ira Flatow, Science Friday, *NPR*, May 11, 2012, http://www.sciencefriday.com/segments/the-case-for-a-presidential-science-debate/.

180 Edward W. Lempinen, "Vernon Ehlers, Congressman and Physicist, Urges Scientists and Engineers to Join the Political Process," *AAAS News*, June 2, 2010, http://www.aaas.org/news/vernon-ehlers-congressman-and-physicist-urges-scientists-and-engineers-join-political-process.

181 Edward W. Lempinen, "Vernon Ehlers, Congressman and Physicist, Urges Scientists and Engineers to Join the Political Process," *AAAS News*, June 2, 2010, http://www.aaas.org/news/vernon-ehlers-congressman-and-physicist-urges-scientists-and-engineers-join-political-process.

182 Vernon J. Ehlers. "Challenges for Undergraduate Science Education," *Research and Excellence at Undergraduate Institutions: Annual Report* (2000), 22, Box 67, Folder 36, Ehlers Vernon J. Collection # 525. Heritage Hall Calvin College Archives.

183 Jonathan Hirte (DC Staffer), interview with the author, May 20, 2017.

184 Vernon J. Ehlers, "Editorial: Science Education and Our Nation's Future" *BioScience* 50, no 9, (September 2000), 731, http://www.bioone.org/doi/pdf/10.1641/0006-3568%282000%29050%5B0731%3ASEAONS%5D2.0.CO%3B2.

185 Vernon J. Ehlers, "Are we Scientifically literate" (statement), April 22, 1998, Box 38 Folder 18, Ehlers Vernon J. Collection # 525. Heritage Hall Calvin College Archives. Statement discusses the results of the Third International Math and Science study.

186 "Text of Representative Vernon Ehlers' Remarks to Science Roundtable" (October 23, 1997), Box 9, Folder 2, Ehlers Vernon J. Collection #525. Heritage Hall Calvin College Archives.

187 News from Congressman Vernon J. Ehlers. "Ehlers: President's Space Vision Inspiring But Perilous," press release, January 14, 2004, Box 43, Folder 12, Ehlers Vernon J. Collection # 525. Heritage Hall Calvin College Archives.

188 News from Congressman Vernon J. Ehlers. "Ehlers: President's Space Vision 'Inspiring' But 'Perilous, press release,'" January 14, 2004, Box 43, Folder 12, Ehlers Vernon J. Collection # 525. Heritage Hall Calvin College Archives.

189 News from Congressman Vernon J. Ehlers. "Ehlers Gives 'Two Thumbs Up' to No Child Left Behind Bill," press release, March 22, 2001, Box 43, Folder 8, Ehlers Vernon J. Collection # 525. Heritage Hall Calvin College Archives.

190 "Provisions of Ehlers' Bills on Science and Math Education," *FYI: The American Institute of Physics Bulletin of Science Policy News* 41, April 17, 2000, https://www.aip.org/fyi/2000/provisions-ehlers-bills-science-and-math-education.

191   "H.R. 2272 (110th): America COMPETES Act," Govtrack.us, Accessed August 3, 2016 https://www.govtrack.us/congress/bills/110/hr2272/summary.

192   "Gold star for Ehlers" *Grand Rapids Press Region Section*, August 12, 2007, Grand Rapids History and Special Collections, Grand Rapids Public Library.

193   "Gold star for Ehlers" *Grand Rapids Press Region Section*, August 12, 2007, Grand Rapids History and Special Collections, Grand Rapids Public Library.

Chapter 7

194   Monica Scott. "Ehlers says he's stepping aside," *Grand Rapids Press*, February 10, 2010, Box 62, Folder 8, Ehlers Vernon J. Collection # 525. Heritage Hall Calvin College Archives.

195   Jeff Cranson. "We can learn from Vern," *Grand Rapids Press*, February 11, 2010, Box 62, Folder 8, Ehlers Vernon J. Collection # 525. Heritage Hall Calvin College Archives.

196   Jeff Cranson. "We can learn from Vern," *Grand Rapids Press*, February 11, 2010, Box 62, Folder 8, Ehlers Vernon J. Collection # 525. Heritage Hall Calvin College Archives.

197   Jonathan Hirte (DC Staffer), interview with the author, May 20, 2017.

198   Julia Jester (DC Staffer), interview with the author, July 14, 2017.

199   Andrew Krietz. "Vern Ehlers 'a true statesman,' Says Sen Carl Levin at new Amtrak station's opening," *Mlive.com.* 27 October 2014. http://www.mlive.com/news/grand-rapids/index.ssf/2014/10/vern_ehlers_a_true_statesman_s.html.

200   To Lyle Barber From Vern Ehlers, July 11, 1966. Box 16, Folder 8, Ehlers Vernon J. Collection # 525. Heritage Hall Calvin College Archives.

201   To Lyle Barber From Vern Ehlers, February 19, 1976. Box 16, Folder 8, Ehlers Vernon J. Collection # 525. Heritage Hall Calvin College Archives. This is the latest Lyle letter in the collected correspondence.

202   Jo Ehlers (Vernon Ehlers's wife), in interview with the author, July 7, 2017.

203   Marg Ed Conn. "The Calvin Connection: Making Room for Politics," *West Michigan Magazine*, December 1980, 30. Box 12, Folder 3. Ehlers Vernon J. Collection # 525. Heritage Hall Calvin College Archives.

204   Frederick Buechner, *Wishful Thinking*. New York: HarperCollins, 1993.